Follow Your Taste Buds

Contents

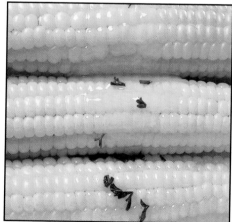

Microwave How To & Tips

Maybe you'll be a better microwave cook if we tell you a little about how a microwave works and give you some cooking hints. Microwaves, as their name implies, are very tiny waves. They are non-ionizing, electromagnetic waves. The waves are so small they can be contained in the walls of your microwave. A magnetron broadcasts a microwave signal when you turn on your microwave, and the signal is converted to heat in your food. When the microwave energy activates the particles in your food, they bounce about 2 1/2 billion times per second. This friction between particles causes heat in the food.

Now that you know a little bit more about how microwaves heat your food, you'll understand the importance of certain microwave cooking processes. Here are some tips and tricks that will bring you one step closer to mastering the art of microwave cooking.

Cut food into uniform pieces. Microwaves can only penetrate 2 inches. So little pieces of food cook faster than larger ones. Cutting uniform pieces will cook food evenly.

Cook cakes and breads in ring pans. Microwaves cannot penetrate to the center of a large cake pan, but they can penetrate to the center of a ring pan. The waves penetrate from all sides fully cooking the cake.

Eat breads immediately. Microwave breads tend to turn hard if not eaten soon after cooking. So don't make muffins the night before and expect to eat them for breakfast. They may turn into cute little bricks if you wait too long.

Stir food from the outside in. The food on the outside of the dish heats up faster than the food in the center. Always stir food from the outside edges of the dish to the inside of the dish to help food cook evenly.

Don't expect golden brown foods. Microwaves do not brown foods, so if you want browned foods you have to cheat.
- Brush meats with a browning sauce before cooking.
- Frost and butter cakes and breads to cover the fact that they aren't brown.
- Use a garnish to detract from the color.
- If all else fails, brown foods for a few minutes in a conventional oven, it's all right, we did it.
- Use browning dishes to brown foods. These dishes are coated with a substance that causes the surface to become extremely hot. Food placed in a preheated browning dish is browned.

Arrange food with the thickest parts towards the outside. For example when cooking chicken arrange the meat so the fleshy parts are on the outer edges of the dish. This will help the food cook evenly because the thick pieces need more heat energy than the thin pieces.

Rearrange food from the outside in. The pieces of food around the outside of the dish heat faster than the pieces on the inside. To help food cook evenly, rearrange food from the outside in several times while cooking.

Always follow directions for stand time. When you microwave, stand time is very important because the heat is in the food, and not in the oven. While the food is standing, it continues to cook, the particles are still bouncing around from when they were set into motion by the microwaves. So don't skip this step, it's very important.

Always use microwave-safe dishes. Here's a test to see if a dish is microwave-safe. Place the dish you are testing in the microwave with a cup of water. Microwave on high for 1 minute. If the dishes are cool enough to handle, they are microwave-safe. If they are very hot, do not use them in the microwave.

Garnishing with Fruit

1. Make 3 even slices in the strawberry without cutting through the top of it.

2. Carefully fan the strawberry slices without detatching them from the stem.

3. Garnish cakes, breads, or salads with the strawberry fan.

Substitutions & Temperatures

Given Ingredient	Substitute	Microwave Power Levels
1 tablespoon cornstarch	2 tablespoons flour	100% = HIGH
1 egg	2 egg yolks	75% = MEDIUM HIGH
1 ounce chocolate	3 tablespoons cocoa and 1 tablespoon butter	50% = MEDIUM
1 tablespoon fresh snipped herbs	1 teaspoon dried herbs	30% = MEDIUM LOW
1 fresh onion	1 tablespoon rehydrated instant onion	10% = LOW
1 teaspoon dry mustard	1 tablespoon prepared mustard	
1 clove garlic	1/8 teaspoon garlic powder	
1 shallot	1 clove garlic	
oil	applesauce	
sugar	honey	
wine, brandy, sherry	apple juice	
scallions	green onions	
ricotta cheese	cottage cheese	
butter	margarine	

Deveining shrimp

1. Rinse with water and slice down the outer rim of the shrimp with a sharp knife.

2. Carefully pull out the exposed veins and discard them.

3. Rinse the shrimp thoroughly.

Garnishing with Chocolate Leaf

1. Wash a rose or lemon leaf (others may be toxic) and spread melted chocolate on it.

2. Place the leaf on wax paper in the freezer to harden. Peel the leaf from the chocolate.

3. Garnish cakes and desserts with the chocolate leaf.

Appetizers

The Ultimate Taco Dip

You know it's August when you're afraid to answer your door because it may be more neighbors bearing gifts of zucchini. Well, if you do end up with some zucchini, here is one recipe that actually calls for some.

2 cups shredded zucchini
1 cup cut-up cooked chicken
1/8 teaspoon salt
Dash pepper
1/2 cup chopped green pepper
2 tablespoons sliced green onion
2/3 cup taco sauce
1 cup Monterey Jack cheese

Take your neighbor's zucchini and shred it. Place the zucchini in a 1-quart casserole dish, microwave on high for 3 or 4 minutes, stirring once. When it's tender it is finished, so cover it and let it stand. After 5 minutes, drain it thoroughly by pressing out the excess water.

Spread the zucchini evenly on the bottom of the same dish, and spread the chicken over it. Sprinkle with salt and pepper, then onions and green peppers, and finally pour on the taco sauce. Cover the thing and microwave it on high for 4 to 7 minutes. The exact timing depends on your microwave, but it's done when it's bubbly around the edges.

Now sprinkle with cheese and microwave for a couple more minutes at 70%. Be sure to turn the dish every minute so it will cook evenly. When the cheese is melted the dip is finished. Pull it out of the microwave and serve it with your favorite tortilla chips, or if you're frugal, whichever chips are on sale.

Serves: 6 Prep: 6 Cook: 19 Total: 25

Swiss Cheese Fondue

If you love cheese, this is the appetizer for you—it's good stuff. We're not going to lie to you, this tasty dish is not low fat, but one taste and you'll know it's worth it.

4 cups shredded Swiss cheese
3 tablespoons flour
1/8 teaspoon garlic powder
1 cup dry white wine
Dash nutmeg
Cubed French bread

Get a plastic bag that holds a couple of quarts. One of the *yellow and blue makes green, it's closed!* bags, is probably going to be your best choice because you'll know it's closed, and you won't get fondue fixin's all over the place.

Place the cheese, flour, and garlic into the bag of your choosing and shake it gently. Now heat the wine in the microwave at 50% for 2 to 3 minutes. Don't boil it, but it should be hot.

Now combine everything into one bowl. Microwave the mixture at 50% for 6 to 8 minutes. Vigorously stir with a wire whip every 2 minutes. The fondue is done when it is smooth.

Sprinkle the fondue with nutmeg and serve with the cubes of French bread for dipping.

Serves: 6 Prep: 3 Cook: 11 Total: 14

Spinach Chicken Dip

Before you start this recipe, make sure you really know how to work the power on your microwave. Other than that, the hardest part of this recipe is getting the spinach out of the packaging. Good luck and happy eating.

5 ounces boneless skinless chicken breast
1 10-ounce package frozen chopped spinach
   (make sure it's the chopped kind)
2 tablespoons chopped onion
3 ounces cream cheese
1/2 cup shredded Swiss cheese
1/4 cup mayo (or Miracle Whip if you desire)
1/4 cup sliced black olives
1/4 cup milk
1/2 teaspoon salt
1/8 teaspoon nutmeg
1/8 teaspoon fennel seed, crushed
1/8 teaspoon pepper

Wash off the chicken, because you don't know where it's been. Then place it in a microwave-safe baking dish. If you have a 9-inch round dish use it. Set the microwave power level at 70% and microwave the chicken for 2 to 5 minutes. The exact timing totally depends on your microwave, so check it every few minutes. The chicken is done when it is no longer pink inside and all the juices run clear. Chop or shred the chicken, whichever you choose. Now set the chicken aside for a bit.

Take the frozen spinach out of the poorly designed little cardboard package that it comes in, and place that frozen block of spinach on a plate. Set your microwave on high and cook for 4 to 5 minutes. The spinach should be warm. Drain it thoroughly and set it over by the chicken.

Take a casserole dish and put the onion in it. Microwave on high for 45 seconds, maybe a whole minute if your machine is slow. Just cook until the onion is tender-crisp. This may sound like an oxymoron, but as long as the onion isn't mushy, you're doing fine.

Now dump everything into the casserole dish with the onions. Be sure to mix it up really well. Change the power level down to 70% again, and microwave the whole concoction for about 3 minutes, stirring once. If the whole mess is warm throughout and the cheese is melted it's done.

Taste it to make sure it's alright, and then serve it with crackers or chips.

Serves: 6 Prep: 8 Cook: 15 Total: 23

Guacamole

If you can mash avocados you can make this easy Guacamole. You can also make this ahead of time and freeze it.

4 slices of bacon
2 ripe avocados
1 tablespoon lemon juice
1/2 teaspoon onion salt
1/8 teaspoon chili powder
1 small chopped tomato (for later)

Cover a plate with three layers of paper towels. Arrange the bacon on the paper towels and cover the bacon with another paper towel. Microwave the bacon on high for 3 to 4 minutes. After cooking, let the bacon stand for 3 to 5 minutes, then crumble it.

Now take the avocados, pit them, peel them, and mash them up. Add everything, except the tomato, to the mashed up avocados. Stir until everything is completely mixed. Stir in the chopped up tomatoes, and serve this tasty dip with corn chips.

If you want to freeze the dip for later, don't add the tomatoes. Dump the guacamole into a freezer container. Be sure you label it, so if you forget you will still be able to identify it weeks from now. Toss the container in the freezer and come back when the dip is frozen. Don't leave it in there for more than a month though.

Let's say you come back in two days, and you're ready to finish making this great

guacamole. Take the labeled container out of the freezer and then take the guacamole out of the container. Put that frozen chunk of guacamole into a 1 quart casserole dish. Microwave it at 50% for 4 to 5 minutes, or until defrosted. You might have to break the ice on it after a couple minutes. Stop microwaving when the guacamole is defrosted, but cold.

Now stir in the chopped up tomato and the hibernating guacamole is ready to eat.

Serves: 4 Prep:5 Cook 5 Total: 10

Wonton Fans

You probably never even thought of making wontons in the microwave, but it is in fact possible. The major benefit of making wontons in the microwave is, they aren't deep-fried. It's a major culinary break-through and we are including it in this cookbook just for you.

6 wonton skins cut into 2 x 2-inch squares
2 teaspoons melted butter
Pinch thyme
Pinch oregano
Fresh ground Parmesan cheese

Folding the wontons allows for some creativity. You can fold it into a fan by folding it and dipping one end in water and pinching it. Or just fold the wontons like an accordion. You can even cut them into triangles and leave them flat. Have some fun creating shapes.

Then place a paper towel on a plate and arrange the wontons on the towel. Brush each wonton with the melted butter and sprinkle the thyme and oregano over them.

After you have finished all of the brushing and sprinkling, pop the plate of wonton skins into the microwave. Cook them on high until they are crisp, which will be about 1 1/2 minutes.

Sprinkle the wontons with Parmesan cheese and microwave them for 20 seconds at 50%. When the cheese is melted, they are ready to eat.

Serves: 4 Prep: 6 Cook: 2 Total: 8

Cheese Ball

It seems like there is some unwritten law that says you can only eat a cheese ball at parties. Well, this recipe is so easy that you'll probably start making it just to snack on while you watch TV. But feel free to make it for parties too.

1/4 cup chopped green onion
1/4 cup chopped green pepper
1 teaspoon butter
1 8-ounce package cream cheese
2 cups shredded cheddar cheese
1 4-ounce package crumbled blue cheese
1 tablespoon chopped pimiento
1 teaspoon prepared horseradish
2 teaspoons Worcestershire sauce
1 minced clove garlic
1/2 cup chopped pecans

Place onion, pepper, and butter in a small bowl and microwave on high for 30 to 45 seconds. The vegetables should be cooked just until they are tender. Set this bowl of stuff aside for a minute.

Place the cream cheese in another microwave-safe bowl. Make sure to get all of the foil wrapping off of the cream cheese. Now set the power level at 50% and microwave for one minute or until the cream cheese is softened.

After softening the cream cheese, dump everything except the pecans into the bowl and stir. Keep stirring until everything is sufficiently mixed. Now form all of the mixture into a ball, pyramid, cube, or whatever shape you want. Wrap it in plastic wrap and put it in the fridge for 2 to 3 hours.

After a few hours of chilling the cheese ball, unwrap it, roll it in the pecans, and serve with any type of cracker that seems fit to be served with cheese ball.

Serves: 12 Prep: 3 Cook: 1 Chill: 120
Total: 124

El Nacho Grande

Few other appetizers can please a crowd like this big pile of nachos. It's big and it's delicioso, and that's why we call it El Nacho Grande.

1 cup shredded Monterey Jack cheese
    with jalapeño peppers
1 cup shredded cheddar cheese
1/2 cup diced red onion
1/3 cup sliced black olives
7-ounce bag tortilla chips
Sour cream
Salsa

Combine the cheese, olives, and onion in a bowl and set aside. Then find a 12-inch round microwave-safe platter and arrange about 1/3 of the chips on it. Sprinkle about 1/3 of the cheese mixture over that. Continue making layers of chips and cheese, making sure to end with the cheese mixture on top.

Microwave the layered chips and cheese for 2 to 3 minutes on high. You can top the nachos with sour cream and salsa if you want. Or just serve El Nacho Grande with sour cream and salsa on the side. Either way you'll enjoy this big appetizer.

Serves: 6 Prep: 8 Cook: 3 Total: 11

Breads

Orange Breakfast Ring

This fancy breakfast bread will impress anyone. It's perfect to serve with a Sunday brunch– fast and easy, yet fancy.

Lemon wafers or graham cracker crumbs
1/4 cup sugar
1/2 cup orange juice
1 egg
2 cups buttermilk baking mix
   (kinda like Bisquick)
1/2 chopped pecans
1/2 cup orange marmalade

Glaze:
1 cup powdered sugar
3 tablespoons orange juice
3 tablespoons grated orange peel

Grease a 10 to 12 cup microwave-safe cake ring pan. Coat the pan with as many crumbs as will stick to the greased pan.

In a mixing bowl, beat together sugar, orange juice, and the egg. Stir in the buttermilk baking mix stuff, and then blend until well mixed. Stir in pecans and marmalade until they are evenly mixed.

Pour the batter into the cake ring coated with crumbs. Microwave at 50% for 2 1/2 minutes, rotate the pan, and microwave for 2 1/2 more minutes. Now increase the power level to high and microwave again for 1 to 5 more minutes. Watch the cake, and stop microwaving when there is no more unbaked batter at the bottom of the pan.

Set the pan right-side up on the counter for 5 minutes, and don't mess with it. After five minutes, dump it out onto a plate.

While the bread is standing, make the glaze. Mix all of the glaze ingredients together with a fork, until it is smooth. Then drizzle the glaze over the cake, and it's ready to serve.

Serves: 4 Prep: 8 Stand: 5 Cook:10 Total: 23

Banana Sticky Buns

This is a sticky variation of banana bread muffins. These are a lot easier and faster to make than traditional banana bread muffins. But they are just as good.

4 tablespoons melted butter
2 sliced bananas
1/3 cup shredded coconut
1/2 cup orange marmalade
1 10-ounce package refrigerator biscuits

Melt the butter by microwaving it for 30 seconds on high. Grease a microwave-safe muffin tin (which should not be tin but rather a microwave-safe material) with the melted butter.

Place 3 banana slices in each muffin cup. Drizzle 1 teaspoon of marmalade over the bananas. Sprinkle 1 teaspoon coconut over that, and top it off with 1 flakey biscuit. Brush each biscuit with butter; you're ready to bake the muffins.

Microwave them at 70% for 5 minutes. When they are done dump them out of the muffin tin immediately. They are ready to eat anytime; enjoy. Be careful not to get sticky.

Makes: 10 Prep: 6 Cook: 5 Total: 11

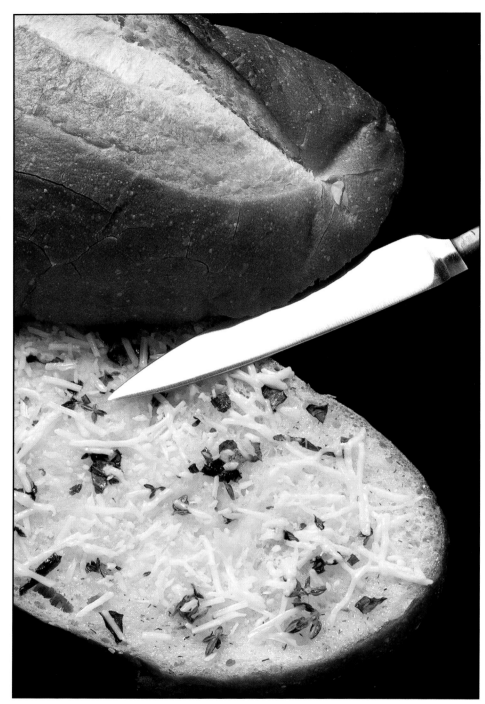

Herbed French Bread

This is a recipe for that yummy French bread you like to eat with Italian food. Instead of just throwing some butter and garlic on your bread, try this recipe. It's just as easy and it tastes even better.

1 loaf French bread.
3/4 cup butter
1 tablespoon basil
1 tablespoon oregano
1 1/2 teaspoons celery seed
3/4 teaspoon onion powder
1/2 cup grated Parmesan cheese

Cut the loaf of French bread in half lengthwise. Place the 2 half loaves on a paper towel and set on a microwave-safe platter.

Put the butter in a small microwave-safe dish and soften by microwaving at 10% for 2 minutes. Then stir the basil, oregano, celery seed, and onion powder into the softened butter. Spread each half of bread with the herbed mixture and Parmesan cheese, and pour the extra over the top of the loaf.

Microwave the bread for 2 minutes or until it is steamy and warm. Slice the bread and serve it in a cute little basket or something.

Serves:10 Prep: 2 Cook: 4 Total: 6

Cinnamon-Nut Muffins

These tasty cinnamon-nut muffins are a delicious breakfast muffin. The cinnamon and nuts makes them an especially good Christmas treat.

3/4 cup flour
1 teaspoon baking powder
1/8 teaspoon salt
1/2 cup finely chopped pecans
1/4 cup packed brown sugar
1/3 cup milk
3 tablespoons oil
1 beaten egg yoke
1 1/2 tablespoons sugar
1 teaspoon cinnamon

Combine the flour, baking powder, salt, nuts, and sugar in a bowl and form a well in the center of the dry ingredients. This means make a little hole in the dry ingredients.

Beat the milk, egg yolk, and oil together, and pour it in the little well that you made. Stir just until everything is moistened. When making muffins it is important that you do not overmix. Now you are ready to bake the muffins.

Line a 6-cup muffin tin with paper muffin liners. The tin will of course not be made of tin, but rather some sort of microwave-safe material. Fill each cup half full of batter.

Microwave the muffins on high for 2 1/2 to 3 1/2 minutes. Rotate the muffin tin every minute or so. The muffins will still be slightly wet to the touch, but they are done cooking.

Melt the butter in a shallow microwave-safe dish, by microwaving it for 30 seconds on high. In another shallow dish, mix the cinnamon and sugar together. Dip the top of each muffin in the melted butter, and then in the cinnamon and sugar mixture.

Your Cinnamon-Nut Muffins are ready to eat anytime now. Enjoy!

Makes: 6 Prep: 7 Cook: 4 Total: 11

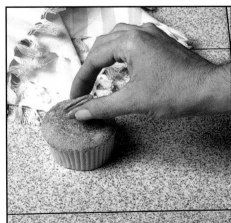

Chili Cheese Corn Bread

This is one of the world's easiest corn bread recipes. All you do is put everything in a bowl and stir. And it only takes a few minutes to cook.

1/2 cup flour
1/2 cup corn meal
1/2 cup corn (frozen or canned)
1/2 cup chopped green peppers
1 tablespoon sugar
2 teaspoons baking powder
1/2 teaspoon salt
1/2 teaspoon chili powder
1/3 cup milk
1 egg
1/4 cup shortening or oil
Red pepper flakes

Place all of the ingredients except the red pepper flakes, in a mixing bowl and mix it by hand. Stir until everything is moistened. Be sure not to overstir. Now you are ready to cook the bread.

Lightly grease a microwave-safe pie plate. Spread the batter in the plate and sprinkle it with red pepper flakes. Microwave for 2 1/2 to 4 1/2 minutes. The bread should be firm on the outside and moist on the inside. Let the bread stand for a couple minutes before serving. See, that was pretty easy. Enjoy your corn bread.

Serves 8 Prep: 5 Cook: 5 Total: 10

Choco-Chip Coffee Cake

Grab a couple cans of refrigerator biscuits and whip up this treat in no time.

1/2 cup sugar
1 teaspoon cinnamon
2 cans flakey refrigerator biscuits
1/2 cup chocolate chips
1/2 cup butterscotch chips
1/2 cup melted butter

Place the cinnamon and sugar in a large plastic bag. Then cut each biscuit into fourths and dump them into the bag. Shake 'em around until each piece is coated with cinnamon and sugar.

Grease a 9-inch round pie plate and arrange the biscuit pieces in the dish. Drizzle the melted butter over the bread and microwave it at 50% for 6 minutes; turn the dish after 3 minutes.

Increase the power to high and microwave for 2 minutes. Sprinkle the cake with the chips and microwave it for 2 minutes. Serve the cake warm and enjoy.

Serves: 8 Prep: 3 Cook: 10 Total: 13

Brown Bread

This makes two loaves of delicious brown bread. Spread the slices of bread with butter for a tasty snack or treat. The best part of this recipe is that it's really easy.

1/2 cup flour
1/2 cup corn meal
1/2 cup whole wheat flour
3/4 cup buttermilk
1/2 cup molasses
1 teaspoon baking soda
1/8 teaspoon salt
3/4 cup raisins

Mix all of the ingredients, except the raisins, with an electric mixer. Mix at a low speed until it's thoroughly blended. Then stir in the raisins, just until they are mixed evenly throughout the batter.

That's all the mixing you have to do. Now you're ready to cook.

Take a 2-cup glass container and grease it a lot. Spoon half of the mixture into the greased dish and cover with wax paper. Microwave at 50% for about 7 minutes. Turn the dish half way after 3 minutes of microwaving. The bread will be done when it is slightly wet to the touch.

Wrap the cooked loaf in plastic wrap so it won't dry out. Now repeat this cooking process with the other half of the batter. Be sure to regrease the dish before cooking the second loaf. Whenever you're ready, the bread is ready to eat.

Makes: 2 loaves Prep: 8 Cook: 7 per loaf Total: 22

Onion Loaf

This onion flavored bread is an excellent choice for a dinner bread. It only takes a few minutes to prepare and cook.

3 tablespoons butter
1/2 cup chopped onion
1 chopped garlic clove
2 tablespoons chopped parsley
1 16-ounce can jumbo refrigerator biscuits

Grease a bread pan and set it aside for a minute. Combine the butter, onion, and garlic in a microwave-safe bowl. Microwave on high for about 3 minutes, just until the onion is tender.

Stir the parsley into the onion mixture, and spread it on one side of each biscuit. Line the biscuits up on their sides in the bread pan. Microwave the loaf at 70% for 8 to 10 minutes. Be sure to turn the loaf every 3 minutes.

When it's done cooking let the loaf stand for about 5 minutes before eating. When you are ready to eat, dump the loaf out onto a plate and serve.

Serves: 8 Prep: 3 Cook: 9 Stand: 5 Total: 17

Whole Wheat Blueberry Muffins

These muffins are high in fiber because of the whole wheat. Even though they are nutritious they are still high in taste. Microwave a batch and take comfort in knowing you're doing something good for your health.

1/2 cup flour
1/2 cup whole wheat flour
2 tablespoons sugar
2 teaspoons baking powder
1/2 teaspoon salt
1 1/2 tablespoons butter
1 1/2 tablespoons vegetable oil
1/2 cup milk
1 slightly beaten egg
1 cup blueberries

Combine all dry ingredients and make a well in the center. For those of you who don't cook too often, a well is just a little hole in the center of the flour and stuff. It's sort of like the swimming pool you make with your mashed potatoes and gravy.

Put the butter in a dish and zap it until it is melted. It should take about 30 seconds. Add the oil, milk, and egg to the melted butter. Pour the mixture into the little well you made. Stir just until the dry ingredients are moistened. Then fold in the blueberries. When making muffins, it's very important not to over mix so just stir until the blueberries are mixed evenly throughout the batter.

To bake the muffins, place paper muffin liners in your microwave-safe muffin tin (which definitely should not be tin.) Fill each cup half full of batter. Microwave on high for 2 to 4 minutes. The muffins will be firm on the outside and moist on the inside. Take them out of the microwave and let them stand for 5 minutes.

These healthy muffins are ready to eat anytime after sitting for five minutes.

Makes: 12 Prep: 9 Cook: 4 Total: 13

Honey Bran Muffins

These honey bran muffins are great for breakfast or as a healthy snack any time of the day. *(Photo opposite page.)*

2 cups boiling water
6 cups all-bran or bran flakes
1 cup honey
1 cup sugar
1 cup packed brown sugar
1 cup shortening
1 tablespoon and 2 teaspoons soda
2 teaspoons salt
4 eggs
5 cups flour
4 cups buttermilk

Put 2 cups of the bran and all of the honey into the boiling water and leave it to soak while you do the other stuff.

In another mixing bowl combine the sugars, shortening, soda, salt, and eggs. Beat everything really well.

Now stir in half of the flour. Be sure to stir it in by hand, because if you use the mixer it's going to fly all over the place. After the flour is mixed in, blend the buttermilk in and stir in the rest of the flour.

All of this time the bran should have been soaking; add it along with the other 4 cups of bran. Blend everything well.

Line a 6-cup muffin tin (which should be made of a microwave-safe material, and not real tin) with muffin papers. Fill each cup half full, and place it in the microwave. Microwave for 3 1/2 to 4 1/2 minutes. The muffins should be firm on the outside, and moist on the inside. Let the muffins stand for a few minutes before serving.

Makes: 12 Prep: 5 Cook: 5 Total: 10

Caramel Sticky Ring

This sticky ring was appropriately named; it's gooey, sticky, caramely, and very delicious. Try it, and in a few minutes you'll be enjoying a tasty caramel treat. *(Photo opposite page, top.)*

1/4 cup butter
1/4 cup packed brown sugar
2 tablespoons corn syrup
1/2 cup chopped pecans
2 10-ounce cans flaky refrigerator biscuits
1 tablespoon sugar
1/2 teaspoon cinnamon

Grease a microwave bundt pan. Sprinkle the brown sugar and nuts in the pan. Pour the syrup over the nuts. Then melt the butter by microwaving it for 1 minute and pour it in the pan as well.

Open the tube of flaky biscuits; cut each one in half and roll them into balls. Combine the cinnamon and sugar and roll each ball in the mixture. Place the balls in the pan so they are touching each other but not stacked on top of each other.

Microwave at 70% for 5 1/2 minutes. Turn the pan after 3 minutes. After the sticky ring is finished cooking, cover it with plastic and let it stand for 5 minutes. When you are ready to eat, dump the ring out on a plate and serve it. Watch out, it's sticky.

Serves: 8 Prep: 5 Cook: 6 Stand: 5 Total: 16

Breakfast Pull-Apart Loaf

This is one of the fastest breakfast breads you can make, not to mention one of the easiest. The hardest part of this recipe is letting the loaf stand before digging in. We think this tangy orange bread will become one of your favorites. *(Photo opposite page, bottom.)*

3/4 cup butter
1/2 cup sugar
1/2 cup orange juice
1 16-ounce package jumbo refrigerator biscuits

Grease a microwave-safe bread pan. Melt the butter by microwaving it for a minute.

Pop open the tube of biscuits and dip each one in the melted butter. Line the biscuits on their side in the greased pan.

Mix the sugar into the orange juice, until it is dissolved. Then pour the juice mixture over the biscuits. Cover the pan of biscuits and microwave at 70% for 7 minutes. Turn the pan around every 2 minutes. When the loaf is done cooking let it stand for 5 minutes. Dump it out on a tray and dig in.

Serves: 8 Prep: 4 Cook: 8 Stand: 5 Total: 17

Soups & Salads

Seafood Pasta Salad

This seafood salad is a good choice for a summer evening meal. It's a tasty, chilled salad full of healthy vegetables and seafood. Be sure to prepare the salad early enough so there is time for the salad to chill for about three hours.

1/2 cup sliced carrots
1/2 cup frozen peas
6 tablespoons Italian dressing
1/4 pound bay scallops
1/4 pound extra small shrimp
    (shelled and deveined)
1/4 teaspoon dried basil leaves
1 cup mushrooms
1/2 cup julienne zucchini
    (cut into 2 x 1/4-inch strips)
1 7-ounce package rotini noodles,
    cooked and cooled
1/2 teaspoon salt
1/8 teaspoon pepper

In a microwave-safe casserole dish, combine carrots, peas, and 1/4 cup of dressing. Microwave on high until the peas are defrosted, and the color of the vegetables brightens. This should be about 2 or 3 minutes. Stir the vegetables after 1 minute. Set them to the side for a while.

In a 9-inch glass dish, combine the scallops and shrimp. Sprinkle them with basil, then cover the dish with plastic wrap. Set the power level on the microwave down to 70%, and cook the seafood for 3 to 5 minutes, stirring every few minutes. The scallops and shrimp will be done when they are opaque (meaning not see through.) Drain off the water and juices, and stir the seafood into the vegetable mixture. Then add the zucchini and mushrooms. Cover the whole mixture and refrigerate it for an hour.

After chilling, mix the rotini noodles into the mixture. Combine the remaining 2 tablespoons of dressing with the salt and pepper, and pour it over the salad. Toss the salad gently to coat everything with dressing.

The salad isn't ready to eat yet. Cover and refrigerate for at least 2 more hours. Now it's ready!

Serves: 8 Prep: 6 Chill: 3 hours Cook: 8
Total: 3 1/2 hours

Manhattan Clam Chowder

Our Manhattan Clam Chowder takes about 35 minutes to prepare. But after tasting this traditional red chowder, you'll know it was worth the time.

5 slices diced bacon
3 small minced onions
2 chopped carrots
2 chopped celery stalks
1 chopped and peeled potato
1 bay leaf
1/4 teaspoon thyme leaves
1 cup water
1 16-ounce can chopped tomatoes
1 10-ounce can diced clams
1/4 teaspoon pepper
Chopped parsley for garnish

Place the diced bacon in a large microwave-safe dish and cover it with a paper towel. Microwave on high for about 5 minutes. Stir it once while cooking.

Add the onions, carrots, celery, potatoes, bay leaf, and thyme to the bacon. Stir everything together and cover the dish. Microwave on high for about 7 minutes. Be sure to stir the vegetables every couple of minutes. Stop microwaving when the vegetables are tender.

Dump the water, tomatoes, clams, and pepper into the vegetable mixture. Stir everything together and cover. Microwave on high for 5 minutes, or until the chowder is hot. Fish out the bay leaf and chuck it. Garnish the chowder with chopped parsley. It's ready to eat.

Serves: 6 Prep: 20 Cook: 17 Total: 37

Cabbage Soup

For all of you skeptical vegetable haters out there, we just want to assure you that this soup is not only edible, but it's very good. Try it, you'll like it.

2 slices chopped bacon
6 cups chopped cabbage
1 onion sliced in half and sliced thinly
1/4 teaspoon dill weed
1/4 teaspoon caraway seeds
1/8 teaspoon pepper
1 1/2 teaspoons salt
4 cups hot water.
4 tablespoons chicken bouillon granules

Place the bacon in a deep 3-quart casserole dish and cover it. Microwave on high for 3 to 5 minutes, just long enough so the bacon begins to crisp.

Add the cabbage, onion, seasoning, and water to the casserole dish. Mix everything together. Cover and microwave on high for 10 minutes. Then add the extra water. Cover again and microwave on high for 8 to 12 more minutes. When the cabbage and the onions are tender, the soup is finished and ready to serve. Enjoy and feel free to eat a lot; it's extremely low fat.

Serves: 6 Prep: 8 Cook: 25 Total: 33

French Onion Soup

This French Onion Soup is pretty easy to make. It tastes like you slaved over the stove for hours, when all you did was hang out by the microwave for a bit.

6 tablespoons butter
4 onions thinly sliced
2 teaspoons flour
1 tablespoon sugar
1 teaspoon dry mustard
2 10 3/4-ounce cans chicken broth
1/4 cup dry white wine
2 teaspoon Worcestershire sauce
1 cup croutons
1/4 cup shredded Parmesan cheese
1 cup mozzarella cheese

In a 3-quart deep casserole dish, melt the butter by microwaving it for 30 seconds on high. Stir in the onions and microwave them on high for 25 to 30 minutes. Yes, we mean minutes and not seconds. Stir the onions every 3 minutes, and when they are finished cooking, they should be brown and caramelized.

Stir the flour, sugar, and mustard into the onions and mix well. Then stir in the broth, wine, and Worcestershire sauce. Mix everything together well, and microwave on high for 7 to 10 minutes. Stir the soup every couple of minutes while microwaving. The soup should be slightly thick and bubbly.

Ladle the soup into 4 serving bowls. Sprinkle each serving with croutons and cheese. Microwave the bowls for about 2 more minutes. The soup is ready to serve when the cheese it melted.

Serves: 4 Prep: 5 Cook: 40 Total: 45

Cheesy Broc Soup

This soup is tasty, healthy, and very easy to make. Cooking it will only take you a few minutes. So you can spend your day doing something other than cooking.

1 10-ounce package of frozen broccoli
1 10 3/4-ounce can condensed cream of mushroom soup
1 1/2 cups milk
1 teaspoon dried chives
1/8 teaspoon pepper
1 cup shredded cheddar cheese

Microwave the broccoli in the packaging for 3 to 5 minutes. Microwave just until the broccoli is defrosted. If you are using broccoli in a bag, be sure to poke a hole in the bag. After defrosting, chop the broccoli into small pieces.

Get a 2-quart microwave-safe casserole dish and dump all of the ingredients in it. Stir everything together. Cover the dish and microwave on high for 6 to 12 minutes. Stir it every couple of minutes, scraping the soup from the sides. When the soup is hot, stir in the cheese. When the cheese is melted, the soup is ready to eat.

Top it with sour cream if you like; it's ready to serve.

Serves: 4 Prep: 5 Cook: 17 Total: 22

Fruit Salad

This is a recipe for those of you who don't like to follow all the rules. You can add any type of fruit you want to this salad. The dressing can also be used on crepes or fresh berries. Go ahead and experiment.

Juice and pulp of 1 lime
1 teaspoon honey
1/2 teaspoon cinnamon
1 teaspoon butter
Dash cardamom
2 drops vanilla extract
Fruits of your choice: kiwi, starfruit, pear...

In a dish, combine lime juice, honey, cinnamon, cardamom, vanilla, and butter. Microwave on high until the butter is melted, 40 seconds. Stir well.

Slice the fruit and pour the dressing over it. Toss to coat all the fruit with dressing. The salad is ready to serve. Enjoy your creation.

Serves: 4 Prep: 5 Cook: 1 Total: 6

Caldillo

For those of you who don't speak Spanish, Caldillo is Mexican Stew, and it's thick and hearty. This stew is good any time of year, but it's especially good on a cold winter's day. Try serving it with warm tortillas.

2 pounds round steak cut into 1-inch cubes
1/2 cup water
1 chopped clove of garlic
1/2 cup chopped onion
1/2 teaspoon chili powder
1/2 teaspoon crushed oregano
2 cups diced potatoes
1/4 cup diced green chilies
1/2 teaspoon salt
1/2 cup salsa
1 1/2 tablespoons flour

Combine the beef, 1/2 cup water, garlic, onions, chili powder, and oregano in a 2-quart casserole dish. Cover with wax paper and microwave at 50% for 10 minutes. Now add the potatoes, chilies, and salt. Cover the dish again, and microwave at 70% for 15 to 20 minutes. Stir the mixture after 8 minutes.

In another bowl combine 1/2 cup water and flour. Mix it well, until it's smooth. No lumps! Stir the water-flour mixture into the meat mixture. Cover and microwave on high for 2 to 3 minutes. When the stew is hot, take it out, stir it, and let it stand for 5 minutes before serving.

The stew is ready to be served. Eat up.

Serves: 4 Prep: 8   Cook: 35 Stand: 5
Total: 48

Taco Salad

This taco salad is more than just a salad, it's a meal. It's also great as a main dish during the hot summer months.

1 pound ground beef
1 diced onion
1/3 cup ketchup
2 teaspoons chili powder
1 teaspoon ground cumin
1/4 teaspoon black pepper
6 cups shredded lettuce
Tortilla chips
2 chopped tomatoes
1 chopped avocado
1/2 cup sliced black olives
Red onion slices
Cilantro

In a plastic colander combine the ground beef and diced onion. Place the colander in a microwave-safe bowl and microwave on high for 5 to 7 minutes, or until the meat is cooked. Stir the meat several times while microwaving so it will cook evenly.

In a medium bowl, mix the cooked meat, ketchup, chili powder, cumin, and pepper. Microwave the mixture for 1 to 2 minutes or until it is hot.

Arrange tortilla chips and 1 1/2 cups of lettuce on each of 4 plates. Top the lettuce with 1/4 of the meat mixture, tomatoes, avocados, and olives. Garnish each salad with slices of red onion and cilantro; the salads are ready to be served.

Serves: 4   Prep: 6 Cook: 9 Total: 15

Chedda' Corn Chowder

Try saying that three times fast! It doesn't take all day to make this chowder, but it's a flavorful soup everyone will love. The good thing about this recipe is it makes tons, so there will be plenty for everyone.

1 tablespoon margarine
1/2 cup chopped onions
2 cups peeled and diced potatoes
1 cup water
1/2 teaspoon dried whole basil
2 cups milk
2 17-ounce cans creamed corn
1 14-1/2 ounce can whole tomatoes, drained and chopped
1 4-ounce can chopped green chiles (do not drain)
1/2 cup diced sweet red pepper
1/2 teaspoon salt
1/8 teaspoon pepper
1 cup shredded cheddar cheese

In a 3-quart microwave-safe casserole dish, microwave the margarine for about 30 seconds, or until melted. Stir in the onion and microwave for about 3 minutes, or until the onion is tender.

Add the potatoes, water, and basil to the onion and margarine. Cover the dish with heavy plastic wrap. Don't use the flimsy stuff, or it will melt. Microwave on high for 12 to 15 minutes, or until the potatoes are tender. Stir the mixture every 5 minutes or so.

Stir in all the other ingredients except for the cheese. Cover the soup and microwave on high for 5 minutes. Stir the soup every 3 minutes and scrape the sides of the dish.

Add the cheese, and microwave the soup at 30% for 5 or 6 minutes. Stir it after 3 minutes. The chowder is finished when the cheese has melted. It's ready to eat, so serve it immediately.

Serves: 8 Prep: 8 Cook: 30 Total: 38

Mushroom Lovers' Soup

If you love those cute little fungi commonly referred to as mushrooms, you'll love this soup. It has lots of mushrooms, and it's for people just like you. That's why we call it Mushroom Lovers' Soup.

1/2 pound sliced mushrooms
3 tablespoons butter
2 cups chicken stock
3 chopped scallions
2 tablespoons minced parsley
1 chopped shallot or 1 clove minced garlic
1/4 teaspoon tarragon
1 cup cooked wild rice
1 cup half and half
3 teaspoons lemon juice
1/4 teaspoon salt
1/8 teaspoon pepper
Mushroom slices for garnish

Put the mushrooms and butter in a casserole dish and cover. Microwave on high for 5 minutes, stirring after 2 minutes.

Add the stock, scallions, shallot, and spices. Stir everything together and cover with plastic wrap. Poke a few holes in the plastic wrap with a fork. Microwave on high for 2 1/2 minutes, until the soup is nice and piping hot.

Now you need to make a roux (you pronounce the word *roo*.) All you do is melt 4 tablespoons of butter in a microwave-safe dish. Then stir 1/2 cup of flour in with a wire whisk. When the roux is smooth and paste-like stir it into the bowl of hot mushrooms and spices.

Microwave the whole mixture for 3 minutes, and then stir in the half and half, lemon juice, salt, and pepper. The soup is now ready to eat. Enjoy, all you mushroom lovers out there.

Serves: 4 Prep: 10 Cook: 8 Stand: 5 Total: 23

Hot Chicken Salad

This is not your typical chicken salad. But then again, this is not your typical cookbook. This salad is ideal for big groups, because it feeds 8 people. To speed up preparation, the chicken can be cooked and refrigerated ahead of time.

1 chopped onion
1 chopped green pepper
1/4 cup butter
4 cups cooked and cubed chicken
3/4 cups sliced almonds
1/3 cup seasoned bread cubes
2 teaspoons chicken bouillon granules
1/2 teaspoon salt
1/4 teaspoon pepper
1/4 cup Brandy
1/8 cup water
1/8 teaspoon red pepper sauce
3 cups shredded lettuce
3/4 cup halved seedless red grape

In a 3 quart casserole dish combine the butter, onion, and pepper. Microwave on high for 3 to 5 minutes, or until the vegetables are tender, yet crisp.

Stir in the remaining ingredients except for the lettuce and grapes, of course. Microwave on high for 5 to 8 minutes until the whole salad is hot. Then stir in the lettuce and grapes. The salad is ready to serve. It may not be your typical salad, but it's pretty tasty.

Serves: 8 Prep: 5 Cook: 13 Total: 18

Vegetables

Stuffed Bell Peppers

Peppers stuffed full of our seasoned mixture are sure to be a family favorite. Stuffed peppers can be a side dish for you big eaters or an entree for you little eaters. In either case, they are a healthy dish. These peppers are so tasty that skeptical vegetable eaters won't even know they're eating greens.

1 pound extra lean ground beef
1 chopped onion
1 chopped tomato
1 cup cooked rice
1 teaspoon prepared horseradish
4 large peppers
1 slice mozzarella cheese

Wash the peppers, chop off the top and take out the seeds and pulp. Don't save it, you definitely won't need it. Set the peppers to the side for just a minute.

Crumble the ground beef into a bowl and mix it together with the onion, tomato, rice, and horseradish. After stirring the mixture well, stuff 1/4 of it into each pepper. If you buy mutant peppers you might need to use a few wooden toothpicks to stabilize them. Poke the picks around the bottom of the pepper to form a square base. It should look a little like a space probe or something.

Place the peppers on a microwave roasting rack and cover them with wax paper. Microwave on high for 13 to 17 minutes. The peppers should be tender and the meat should no longer be pink.

Top each pepper with some cheese strips. You can arrange the cheese nice and cute if you're aiming to impress people.

Serves: 4 Cook: 17 Prep: 8 Total: 25

Potato Fans

Need a new way to fix potatoes? Looking for a way to jazz up dinner? Try making these fun potato fans. If you can slice a potato, you can make these fans.

1/3 cup grated Parmesan cheese
1 1/2 teaspoons dried parsley flakes
1/4 teaspoon garlic powder
1/4 teaspoon onion salt
1/4 teaspoon paprika
6 baking potatoes
1/4 cup plus 2 tablespoons butter
Lemon slices and parsley sprigs for garnish

In a small bowl, mix the first 5 ingredients. Set this little bowl of fixin's over to the side.

Now wash the potatoes and pat them dry. Slice the potatoes crosswise into 1/4-inch thick slices. Do not cut all the way through the potatoes or you'll mess it up. Try to make the potato look like a fan. If you do cut all the way through the potato, just get a new one. After all of the potatoes are cut into fans, soak them in ice water for 10 minutes, then drain.

Melt the butter by microwaving it on high for about 30 seconds. Arrange the potatoes in a 13 x 9 x 2-inch dish. Brush each potato with melted butter. Cover the dish with heavy plastic wrap. Use the heavy stuff or else it will melt. Now microwave the potatoes for 20 to 24 minutes, or until they are tender. Rearrange the potatoes every 5 minutes so they will cook evenly. Each time you stop the microwave, brush the potatoes with butter.

After 20 minutes of microwaving, sprinkle the potatoes with the seasoning mixture you made earlier. Cover the dish again and let it stand for about 5 more minutes.

You can garnish the potatoes with lemon wedges and parsley sprigs. But you don't have to—you decide. Whatever you do, you'll enjoy the potatoes.

Baby Carrots

Very fast, very easy, and very tasty. This recipe is for those who don't like to eat their vegetables. These sweet baby carrots are almost irresistible.

1 tablespoon butter
2 tablespoons honey
1/2 teaspoon lemon juice
1 16-ounce can carrots
Slivered almonds

Place the butter in a 1-quart casserole dish. Microwave on high for 30 seconds. Mix in the honey and the lemon juice. Then drain the carrots and stir them into the butter mixture.

Microwave the carrots on high for 2 to 3 minutes. Stir after one minute. When the carrots are warm, pull them out of the microwave, sprinkle with slivered almonds, toss them on the table, and enjoy.

Serves: 4 Prep: 3 Cook: 4 Total: 7

Serves: 6 Cook: 24 Prep: 15 Stand: 5 Total: 44

Stuffed Zucchini

Yet another recipe to help you use up all the zucchini you come across when everyone starts harvesting their gardens. This stuffed zucchini can be used as a side dish or an entree.

1 slice bacon
2 zucchini
1/4 cup chopped onion
1/4 teaspoon basil leaves
1/8 teaspoon black pepper
1/4 teaspoon garlic powder
1 tablespoon grated Parmesan cheese
Dash cayenne pepper
1/2 cup chopped tomato
1 slice thin bread, toasted and crumbled

Slice the zucchini in half lengthwise. Scoop out the inside to form a 1/4-inch shell. It doesn't have to be perfectly even unless you are trying to impress someone. Just make sure you do not break through the skin. Save the zucchini pulp (the guts.) You'll need it later.

Put the bacon on a plate covered with 3 paper towels. Cover the bacon with another paper towel and microwave on high for about 1 minute. When the bacon is crisp, crumble it.

Chop the zucchini pulp that you saved, and mix it together with the bacon, onion, basil, black pepper, garlic, Parmesan cheese, cayenne pepper, tomato, and bread. Spoon the mixture into each scooped-out zucchini half. Each one should be totally full to overflowing. Put the zucchini in a 12 x 8-inch baking dish. Microwave on high for 6 to 8 minutes. You probably already know this, but do not over cook the zucchini or it will be too soft and mushy.

When the zucchini is soft, sprinkle with Parmesan cheese. It is ready to serve. Enjoy your creation.

Serves: 2 Prep: 6 Cook: 9 Total: 15

Corn on the Cob

Believe it or not, this is a recipe for corn on the cob. It may seem too easy, but it tastes best when prepared in the microwave shortly after being snagged off of the stalk. So try it; you'll like it.

Corn on the cob
Butter
Salt and Pepper

All you will need is a cob of corn still in the lovely green husk nature provided for it. Arrange the corn cobs on the floor of the microwave so they are evenly apart. Don't let any of the cobs touch each other. Now nuke 'em for a few minutes. Be sure to turn them every once in awhile so they cook evenly. For 1 cob, microwave 4 minutes. Two cobs will take 8 minutes, 3 cobs will take 11 minutes, and 4 cobs 15 minutes.

Mushrooms with Garlic Butter

Attention all mushroom lovers, here's another recipe just for you. In no time you can be enjoying a serving of tasty mushrooms.

1/4 cup butter
2 minced garlic cloves
12 ounces sliced fresh mushrooms
1/4 teaspoon salt
1/8 teaspoon pepper

Combine the butter and garlic in a 2-quart casserole dish. Microwave this mixture for 2 1/2 to 3 1/2 minutes. After 1 minute stir the garlic. Continue microwaving until the garlic is browned.

Add the salt, pepper, and mushrooms to the browned garlic and butter. Stir the mushrooms a few times until they are coated with the spices and butter. Cover the dish with wax paper and microwave for 3 to 5 minutes. Stir the mushrooms every few minutes.

When the mushrooms are cooked to your satisfaction, take them out and serve them along with something like steak. Or you can just eat them plain if you prefer. Either way, enjoy.

Serves: 4 Prep: 4 Cook: 4 Total: 8

(Corn on the Cob continued.)
After cooking, cover the ears tightly and let them stand for 5 minutes. Now shuck them following these directions. Hold the end of the cob with a paper napkin so you won't torch your hands. If you have hands of steal you can just hold it in your bare hand. Pull back the leaves and watch out for the steam. When the leaves are out of the way, yank the silk straight off.

Season the corn with butter, salt, and pepper and it's ready to eat. Watch out, it's hot! So you might want to dig up those corn holders Aunt Stella gave you and actually use them.

Serves: 1 Prep: 1 Cook: 5 Total: 6

Creamy Shroomy Broccoli

Broccoli spears smothered with rich and creamy mushroom sauce is a great way to prepare broccoli. Try this recipe next time you want to spruce up some broccoli.

2 8-ounce packages frozen broccoli spears
1/4 cup water
1/4 cup chopped green onions
1 tablespoon butter
1 3-ounce package cream cheese
1 10 3/4-ounce can cream of mushroom soup
1/4 teaspoon salt
1/8 teaspoon pepper
1/8 teaspoon paprika

Dump the broccoli and the water into a 2-quart casserole dish. Microwave on high for 7 to 9 minutes. The broccoli should be tender. Drain the extra water off and rearrange the broccoli spears in an 8 x 8-inch dish. Lay them so that every other one is in the opposite direction, like sardines.

Microwave the onion and the butter in a 2-quart casserole dish for about 2 minutes on high, just until the onion begins to become tender. Set the onion aside.

In another 2-quart microwave-safe dish, microwave the cream cheese on high for 30 to 60 seconds. Don't melt the cream cheese, but it should be softened. Mix together the cream cheese, onions, soup, and salt and pepper.

Pour the mixture over the broccoli spears. Sprinkle with paprika. Cover the dish with wax paper and microwave on high for 5 to 7 minutes. Turn the dish half way around after about 3 minutes. The dish is done when everything is thoroughly heated.

Take the wax paper off, place the dish on the table, and it is ready.

Serves: 5 Cook: 18 Prep: 5 Total: 23

Twice-Baked Potatoes

Everybody loves twice-baked potatoes, but they take forever to make in the oven. Since you don't have forever, we decided to include this microwave recipe.

4 large baking potatoes
3/4 cup milk
1/4 cup butter
1/4 cup shredded cheddar cheese

Scrub the potatoes and stab each one a couple of times with a fork. Arrange the potatoes on a paper towel in the microwave. Microwave 'em on high for 8 to 12 minutes.

When they are cool enough to handle, cut lengthwise. Scoop out the insides, leaving a thin shell. Add the milk and butter to the scooped-out potato, and mash.

After mixing and mashing the potato, return 1/4 of the mashed potatoes to each shell. Sprinkle with salt, pepper, and shredded cheese. Microwave for 1 to 2 minutes. When the cheese is melted, they are ready to eat.

Serves: 4 Cook: 14 Prep: 5 Total: 19

Artichokes with Lemon Butter

Maybe you used to eat artichokes because they are pretty cool looking. This recipe for artichokes with lemon butter gives you one more reason to eat them. Do we need to mention that they are healthy, too?

4 artichokes
Lemon juice
1/2 cup water

Lemon Butter:
1/2 cup butter
3 tablespoons lemon juice
1 tablespoon chopped fresh thyme, or
   1 teaspoon dried whole thyme

There's a special technique for washing an artichoke. Plunge it up and down in water until it's clean. Now get ready to do some trimming. Cut about 1/2 inch off the top of the artichoke. Cut off the stem. Pull off the dead leaves. Cut off about 1/4 of each leaf with scissors.

After fully trimming the artichokes, rub them with lemon juice and place them in a 12 x 8 x 2-inch baking dish. Pour the water in and cover the dish with plastic wrap. Make sure to use the heavy duty kind that won't melt. Microwave on high for 10 to 13 minutes. Rearrange the artichokes every 5 minutes. When the leaves pull out easily, they are done. Set the dish aside and quickly make the lemon butter.

Mix all the ingredients together and microwave on high until the butter is melted. Stir the lemon butter and serve it with the artichokes.

Serves: 4 Prep: 12 Cook: 13 Total: 25

Steamed Oriental Vegetables

This dish is an excellent choice for five people looking for a healthy meal. Surprisingly, this potpourri of steamed vegetables only takes a few minutes of preparation. *(Photo opposite page, bottom.)*

1 tablespoon toasted sesame seeds
4 cups fresh bean sprouts
1 7-ounce jar baby corn
1 green pepper cut into 1/4-inch strips
1 cup sliced fresh mushrooms
1 cup pea pods
4 tablespoons Teriyaki sauce

Spread the sprouts out on a 12-inch round plate. Top with pepper, mushrooms, and the baby corn (like the ones Tom Hank eats in the movie Big.) Pour the Teriyaki sauce over the pile of vegetables. Cover with plastic wrap and poke a few holes in it with a fork. Microwave on high for 6 to 9 minutes. Turn the plate half way around after a few minutes of microwaving. When the pepper is tender, the dish is cooked.

Remove the plastic, sprinkle with sesame seeds, and this dish of steamed vegetables is ready for the partaking.

Serves: 5 Cook: 9 Prep: 5 Total: 14

Asparagus with Orange Butter

Don't let the name of this scare you off. It's as easy to make as it is to eat. You can fix this as a side dish to liven up any meal.

1 pound asparagus
2 teaspoons butter
1/4 teaspoon grated orange peel
Pinch thyme

Break the tough ends off the asparagus spears. Peel a couple strips of the skin off each spear. Doing it this way helps the asparagus microwave better. Arrange the asparagus on a plate, in a starburst design with the tips toward the center. Cover with plastic wrap and poke a few holes in it with a fork. Microwave the asparagus on high for 5 minutes, then let it sit for 2 minutes.

While the asparagus is sitting, prepare the orange butter. Microwave the butter, orange peel, and thyme for 30 seconds, or until the butter is melted. Toss the asparagus in with the orange butter. Now it's ready to serve. That was pretty easy, right?

Serves: 4 Prep: 3 Cook: 5 Stand: 2 Total: 10

Main Dishes

Lo Mein

This is an Americanized microwave version of a dish called Lo Mein or Yaki Soba. You can serve it over steamed rice, or just eat it plain. Either way it's a tasty dish.

2 packages chicken ramen noodles
2 cups cabbage (preferably Nappa cabbage)
1 cup diagonally sliced carrots
4 diagonally sliced green onions

1/2 pound sliced fresh mushrooms
3 chopped garlic cloves
1/2 cup water
1/3 cup steak sauce

Cook the ramen according to the package directions, but do not add the seasoning packets. Drain the noodles and set them aside for a minute.

Combine all the other ingredients, except the steak sauce, in a microwave-safe bowl. Microwave on high for 3 minutes, until the vegetables are tender. Stir in the steak sauce. If you like your food spicy, add more steak sauce. Toss the vegetables together with the ramen noodles.

The dish is ready to serve. That was pretty easy to make, right? Enjoy your meal.

Serve: 4 Prep: 7 Cook: 3 Total: 10

Double Cheese Linguine

Do you like cheese? If you do, you'll love this because it's double cheese. You can use this dish as a side dish, or if you really love cheese, serve it as the main dish.

1 7-ounce package linguine
1 cup chopped zucchini
1 cup frozen baby peas
3 tablespoons butter
3 eggs
1/4 cup half and half
1/4 teaspoon salt
1 cup finely shredded mozzarella cheese
1/2 cup grated Parmesan cheese
Tomato wedges

Cook and drain the linguine noodles according to the package directions. Then set them aside. To save time, continue with the rest of the recipe while the noodles cook.

In a 2-quart casserole dish combine the zucchini, peas, and butter. Microwave this dish of vegetables for about 6 minutes on high, stirring it every now and then. The vegetables are finished cooking when they are tender, so set them aside.

Use a whisk to mix together the eggs, half and half, and the salt. Then combine the egg mixture, linguine, cheeses, and vegetables. Toss everything together until mixed thoroughly.

Microwave the whole dish of stuff on high for 6 to 8 minutes. Stir and toss the food every couple of minutes. When the mixture is set, it's done. You can sprinkle the pasta with a little freshly ground pepper if you have any, and garnish with tomato wedges. This cheese lovers' linguine is now ready to serve.

Serves: 4 Prep: 10 Cook: 8 Total: 18

Wild Rice Medley

This recipe is for all of you who like to eat healthy, or at least those of you who are striving to eat healthy. But even if you aren't into "healthy" food and stuff, you'll probably like this because it's very tasty. *(Photo on previous page.)*

3/4 cup uncooked wild rice
3/4 cup uncooked long grain rice
4 cups hot water
1/2 cup chopped onion
1/2 cup finely chopped celery
1/2 cup finely chopped carrots
1/4 cup butter
8 ounces fresh sliced mushrooms
1 tablespoon instant chicken
    bouillon granules

Rinse the rice off in a wire strainer, because you never know what could be in there. Then, in a 5-quart casserole dish, combine the water and the rice. Cover the dish with heavy plastic wrap and microwave on high for 30 to 35 minutes. Stir the rice with a fork every 10 minutes. After 30 minutes the rice should be tender and fluffy. Cover the cooked rice and let it stand for 15 minutes.

In a 2-quart casserole dish, combine the onion, celery, carrots, and butter. Microwave the vegetables on high for 2 to 4 minutes, until the onion becomes tender. Stir in the mushrooms and the bouillon. Microwave for 2 to 3 more minutes, or until everything is hot.

Drain the cooked rice and rinse it in hot water. Toss the vegetables in with the rice and mix everything together. Cover the rice medley, and microwave it for 3 to 4 more minutes. When everything is hot, it is ready to serve.

Serves: 8 Prep: 5 Cook: 47 Total: 52

Vegetable Lasagna

If you don't like meat, or if you really love vegetables, this recipe is for you. Hopefully your friends and family are veggie lovers too, because this makes enough for eight, or one really hungry vegetarian. Don't let the long list of ingredients scare you, this is still pretty easy to make.

16 lasagna noodles
1 cup ricotta cheese
1 cup drained cottage cheese
2 eggs
1/2 cup Parmesan cheese
1/2 teaspoon salt
1/4 teaspoon pepper
1 cup chopped red pepper
1 cup chopped green pepper
1 chopped onion
2 minced garlic cloves
2 tablespoons olive oil
1 grated carrot
1 grated zucchini
1 16-ounce can whole tomatoes
1 6-ounce can tomato paste
1/3 cup red wine
2 teaspoons parsley flakes
2 teaspoons salt
2 teaspoons sugar
1 teaspoon basil
1 teaspoon oregano
2 bay leaves
3 cups grated mozzarella

Cook the lasagna noodles according to the package directions. Then put the noodles in cold water and set them aside.

In a bowl that doesn't have to be microwave-safe, combine the ricotta cheese, cottage cheese, eggs, Parmesan cheese, salt, and pepper. Stir until the ingredients are mixed and set the bowl aside.

Then in a microwave-safe bowl combine the peppers, onion, garlic, and oil. Microwave the vegetables for 5 to 6 minutes, until the vegetables are tender. Stir the carrot and zucchini into the cooled vegetables. Set the bowl aside for a bit.

Smash the tomatoes a little with a fork. Then stir in the tomato paste and the wine, until the mixture is pretty smooth. You can substitute water or grape juice for the wine, just use whatever you have handy. Mix in the parsley, salt, sugar, basil, oregano, and bay leaves. Microwave the mixture on high for 10 minutes. Fish out the bay leaves and chuck them.

Grease a 9-inch dish and fill it with 1 cup of tomato sauce. Now you are ready to start assembling the lasagna rolls.

Drain the noodles and pat them dry as you need them. Lay 2 noodles end to end and overlap them about an inch. Spread the noodles with the ricotta mixture, then cover the ricotta with vegetables, sprinkle with cheese, and spoon some tomato sauce over the cheese. Now you're ready to roll it up. You will have more luck if you don't overload the noodles with filling.

To form the rolls, start at one end and roll the noodle like a sleeping bag. When you get to the end, secure it with a wooden toothpick. Place the rolls in a ring around the outer edge of the dish. Do not place any rolls in the center of the dish.

Microwave the rolls for 5 minutes, then let them stand for 10 minutes to set before eating. If you think making the lasagna rolls seems like too much trouble, you can make a pan of lasagna with this same recipe. Cover the bottom of the dish with noodles and make layers of ricotta, vegetables, mozzarella, and sauce. End with a layer of mozzarella cheese on top.

Whichever way you decide to cook your lasagna, you'll enjoy it. It's great rolled up, or straight out of the pan.

Serves: 8 Prep: 20 Cook: 23 Stand: 10
Total: 53

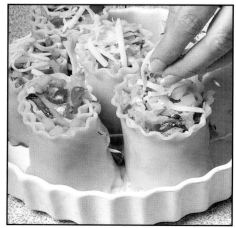

Fried Rice

You've probably never made fried rice in the microwave, but it's possible. In fact, it's very easy. Try it and in a few minutes you'll be enjoying a tasty dinner.
(Photo this page, bottom.)

2 beaten eggs
1 tablespoon water
1/3 cup chopped green onion
1/4 cup chopped red pepper
1/2 cup grated carrots
1 tablespoon oil
3 cups cooked long-grain rice
1/2 cup cooked diced ham
1/2 cup thawed baby peas
2 tablespoons teriyaki sauce

Mix the eggs and water together in a microwave-safe bowl. Cover the bowl with the heavy plastic wrap that won't melt, and microwave on high for 1 1/2 to 2 minutes. Stir after the eggs have microwaved for about 1 minute. When the eggs are set, cut them into 1-inch strips, and set aside.

Put the green onions, red pepper, carrots, and the oil in a 2-quart casserole dish, and microwave it on high for 2 minutes. The onions should be tender but not too soft. Stir the eggs and all the other ingredients in with the onions. Cover the casserole dish with heavy plastic again, and microwave for 2 to 4 minutes.

When the rice is heated all the way through, it is finished. Serve it alongside your favorite Chinese entree, or as the main course.

Serves: 4   Prep: 5   Cook: 6   Total: 11

Basil Tomato Fettuccini

This recipe is for anyone who wants to make a nice dinner quickly. It's delicious, easy, and most importantly, it's fast. Our fresh basil fettuccini is also very elegant. Your guests will never know you microwaved this lovely dish.

2 tablespoons chopped fresh basil
1/2 teaspoon salt
1/4 teaspoon pepper
2 pounds spinach fettuccini noodles
3 tablespoons olive oil
2 chopped tomatoes
2 chopped garlic cloves
Parmesan cheese

Cook the fettuccini noodles according to the package directions. While the noodles cook, continue with the rest of the recipe.

In a microwave-safe dish combine all the ingredients except the Parmesan cheese. Microwave the mixture on high for 3 minutes until it is thoroughly heated. Drain the noodles, toss them together with the basil mixture, and sprinkle Parmesan cheese over the top.

That's about all it takes. Your Basil Tomato Fettuccini is now ready to eat. Don't tell anyone how easy it was.

Serves: 4 Prep: 8 Cook: 3 Total: 11

Confetti Rice

Confetti Rice is rice with little bits of peppers, carrots, and peas. The beauty of this recipe is the fact that it's a microwave recipe. Rice in the microwave—pretty nifty, eh? *(Photo opposite page, top.)*

1 1/2 cups uncooked long grain rice
1 diced carrot
1/4 cup chopped red pepper
2 tablespoons Worcestershire sauce

1/2 teaspoon salt
1/4 teaspoon garlic powder
2 3/4 cups hot water
2 tablespoons chicken bouillon granules
1/2 cup frozen green peas

Place everything except the peas in a 3-quart casserole dish. Mix all of the ingredients together and cover the dish with heavy plastic wrap. Microwave on high for 5

minutes. Then reduce the heat to 50%, recover the dish, and microwave for 15 to 17 minutes until the liquid is gone and the rice is no longer hard. Stir in the peas and microwave for 1 more minute.

Cover the dish and let the rice stand for 5 minutes. It is now ready to serve.

Serves: 5 Prep: 3 Cook: 23 Stand: 5 Total: 31

Fettuccini Alfredo

Cook up a little taste of Italy in a matter of minutes. But don't let an Italian chef know you cooked Italian food in a microwave.

3/4 pound fresh fettuccini
4 tablespoons butter
3 tablespoons flour
2 cups milk
1/4 teaspoon salt
1/8 teaspoon white pepper
Dash cayenne pepper
1 1/2 cups grated Parmesan

Cook the fettuccine according to the package directions. While the noodles are cooking, make the sauce in the microwave. In a 2-quart microwave-safe dish, microwave the butter on high for 1 minute, until it is melted.

Stir in the flour with a wire whisk until it is thoroughly mixed. Add the milk, pepper, salt, and cayenne. Microwave on high for 4 to 5 minutes. Stir the sauce with a wire whisk every 2 minutes. The mixture should be thick and smooth. Stir 1 cup of Parmesan cheese into the hot white sauce until it is melted.

Drain the pasta and toss it with the sauce. Serve the dish with the extra Parmesan cheese on the side.

Serves: 4 Prep: 5 Cook: 6 Total: 11

Southwestern Chili Pie

Who says pie is just for dessert? After you try this Southwestern Chili Pie you'll start eating pie for dinner more often.

1 pound ground beef
1 chopped onion
1/2 cup chopped green pepper
1 minced garlic clove
1 15-ounce can kidney beans
1 4-ounce can tomato sauce
1 envelope taco seasoning
1 package corn bread mix
1 8 1/2-ounce can creamed corn

Crumble the ground beef into a microwave-safe dish with the onion and green pepper. Microwave on high for 5 minutes, stirring every couple minutes. When the meat is finished cooking and the vegetables are tender, stir in the kidney beans, tomato sauce, and taco seasoning. Microwave the mixture on high for 2 to 3 minutes. Set aside for a minute.

Prepare the corn bread mix according to the package directions (but of course don't cook it yet) and stir in the creamed corn. Pour 1/2 of the corn bread batter into a greased 9-inch pie plate. Spoon the meat mixture over the batter, and cover with the rest of the corn bread mix.

Microwave at 50% for 3 minutes. Turn the pie plate and microwave the pie on high for 5 minutes. Let the pie stand for about 3 minutes before eating. Top with sour cream and serve.

Serves: 6 Prep: 10 Cook: 16 Stand: 5
Total: 31

Green Bean Casserole

This recipe is about as easy as they come. Around harvest time you can use fresh green beans, and in the winter, canned green beans work just as well.

1 pound fresh green beans cut into
   1-inch pieces, or 2 15 1/2-ounce
   cans green beans
1/2 cup water
1 10 1/2-ounce can cream of mushroom soup
1 8-ounce can sliced water chestnuts
1/4 cup milk
1 4-ounce can sliced mushrooms
1 3-ounce can French fried onions
1/4 teaspoon salt
Dash pepper

Put the beans and the water into a 2-quart casserole dish and microwave it on high for 9 to 11 minutes, or until the beans are tender. Stir the beans after about 5 minutes. When they are done cooking let them stand for at least 2 minutes before draining off the excess water.

Add the cream of mushroom soup, water chestnuts, milk, mushrooms, salt, pepper, and 1/2 of the onions. Stir everything together and microwave for 3 more minutes. When the casserole is hot, take it out and sprinkle the rest of the onions on top.

The Green Bean Casserole is ready to serve. Now wasn't that about the easiest casserole you have ever made?

Serves: 6 Prep: 2 Cook: 14 Total: 16

Mamita's Fajitas

Everybody loves fajitas, especially ours. The thin strips of meat used in these fajitas are tender, marinated, and very delicious. Be sure to start more than an hour ahead so the meat can marinate.

1 pound top round steak or
     boneless chicken breast
1/2 teaspoon red pepper flakes
1/4 teaspoon oregano
3 mashed garlic cloves
1/4 cup water
1 teaspoon white pepper
1 teaspoon black pepper
1 teaspoon paprika
1 tablespoon lemon juice
1 teaspoon onion powder
1 teaspoon garlic powder
1 1/2 cups chopped tomatoes
1 cup chopped bell pepper
1 1/2 cups chopped onion
1 tablespoon vegetable oil
5 8-inch flour tortillas

Pound the meat on both sides. Then cut the meat across the grain into 1/4-inch thick strips. Dump the meat and all of the fixin's, except the oil and tortillas, into a bowl. Cover the bowl and set it in the fridge to marinate for at least 1 hour. Stir the mixture at least twice an hour.

After the meat is finished marinating, continue with the recipe. Microwave a microwave-safe browning dish on high for 4 minutes. (If the browning dish recommends less time, follow the directions on the dish.) After you heat the dish, remember it's hot! Don't torch your hands.

Place the meat in the heated dish and cover it with wax paper. Punch the power down to 50% and microwave for 6 to 8 minutes. Stir the meat every few minutes, until it is no longer pink. When it's finished cooking set the meat aside for a minute.

In a 2-quart casserole dish combine the oil, vegetables, and marinade. Cover the mixture with wax paper and microwave on high for 5 to 6 minutes, stirring the vegetables after 3 minutes. Make sure you set the power back up to high before cooking the vegetables.

When the vegetables are hot, combine them with the meat. Serve the marinated vegetable meat mixture with warm tortilla shells, and shredded cheese. Enjoy these tasty fajitas.

Serves: 5 Prep: 7 Marinate: 60 Cook: 14
Total: 81

Enchiladas

Enchiladas made extremely easy. If you can operate the microwave, you will be able to whip up a tasty pan of enchiladas in no time.

1 can enchilada sauce (3 cups)
1 pound ground beef
3/4 teaspoon ground cumin
1 1/2 teaspoons onion powder
1/4 teaspoon ground oregano
1 teaspoon garlic powder
1/2 teaspoon salt
12 6-inch corn tortillas
2 tablespoons vegetable oil
1 1/2 cups shredded cheddar cheese
1/2 cup chopped onions
2 cups shredded lettuce
1/2 cup chopped tomatoes
Sour cream

Dump the enchilada sauce into a shallow microwave-safe dish, and microwave it on high for 2 minutes, or until it is hot. Set it aside for a minute while you cook the meat.

Crumble the ground beef into a microwave-safe casserole dish and cover it with wax paper. Microwave the meat on high for 5 to 6 minutes. Stir the meat every couple of minutes. When there is no more pink showing, the meat is done. Drain off any grease and stir in the spices.

Set the meat mixture to the side for a minute also.

Take the tortillas and rub each side with oil. Make 2 stacks of 6 tortillas, and wrap each one in wax paper. Microwave each stack on high for 1 minute.

Grease a 12 x 8-inch microwave-safe dish. Now you're ready to start assembling the enchiladas. Dip a tortilla in enchilada sauce, spoon on 3 tablespoons of meat, sprinkle with onion, sprinkle with cheese, roll it up, and place it seam-side down in the greased dish. Repeat this process with each tortilla. Be sure to save some enchilada sauce, onions, and cheese to sprinkle over the dish of rolled-up enchilada.

Now that you have assembled the enchiladas, you are ready to cook them. Cover the dish with wax paper and microwave the enchiladas at 70% for 6 to 8 minutes. Turn the dish after about 4 minutes. When the enchiladas are hot, and the cheese is melted, they are done cooking.

Let the dish stand for 5 minutes, then top it off with lettuce, tomatoes and sour cream. Now it's ready to serve.

Serves: 6 Prep: 10 Cook: 16 Stand: 5
Total: 31

Greek Pita Sandwiches

Looking for something new to make for dinner? Try these Greek Pitas filled with lamb, turkey, and vegetables; they may become a favorite. Don't let the long lists of fixin's scare you, these pitas are easy.

Yogurt Sauce:
1 8-ounce carton plain yogurt
2 chopped green onions
1/2 teaspoon garlic salt
Cayenne pepper

Meat Mixture:
1/2 pound ground turkey
1/2 pound ground lamb
1 minced garlic clove
1/2 cup water
1 1/4-ounce packet onion soup mix
1 tablespoon olive oil
2 teaspoons parsley flakes
1/2 teaspoon oregano
1/4 teaspoon cayenne pepper
1/8 teaspoon thyme

Toppings:
Shredded lettuce
Chopped tomatoes
Chopped cucumber

Mix all of the yogurt sauce ingredients together and put it in the fridge to chill while you prepare the rest of the food.

Crumble the ground meats into a 2-quart casserole dish with the garlic and mix. Microwave on high for 5 minutes. Stir every 2 minutes, breaking the chunks of meat up as you stir. When the meat is no longer pink it is fully cooked. Drain the grease, and stir in the other meat mixture ingredients. Microwave for 4 minutes.

When the mixture is hot, spoon 1/4 of it into each pita bread. Top with the chopped vegetables and the yogurt sauce.

Serves: 4 Prep: 10 Cook: 10 Total: 20

Chimichangas

Chimichangas are deep-fried burritos. And if there's an easy way to fix them in the microwave, our job is to tell you how. Try our microwave chimichanga recipe and see if you don't like it.

5 8-inch flour tortillas
Vegetable oil
3/4 cup refried beans
1/3 cup enchilada sauce
1/2 cup shredded cheddar cheese
Shredded lettuce
Chopped tomato
Sour cream

Rub both sides of each tortilla with oil. Stack the tortillas and wrap the stack in wax paper. Microwave the tortillas on high for 50 seconds.

Fill a tortilla with 2 tablespoons of beans, 1 tablespoon of sauce, and a sprinkle of cheese. Fold the bottom end up, roll the sides in, and fold the top down. Brush the chimichanga with vegetable oil. Repeat the procedure for each tortilla.

Microwave a microwave-safe browning dish on high for 4 minutes. When the dish is hot, place the chimichangas in it. Cook them on high for 4 minutes. Turn each chimichanga over after 2 minutes.

When the chimichangas are finished cooking, serve them with lettuce, tomatoes, and sour cream.

Serves: 5   Prep: 10   Cook: 4   Total: 14

Chicken & Mushroom Quesadillas

These make an excellent snack, or a light lunch any day.

2 boneless chicken breasts
1/2 cup sliced fresh mushrooms
2 chopped green onions
6 tortillas
1 cup shredded cheese
1 minced garlic clove
1 tablespoon butter

Microwave the chicken breasts on high for 3 to 5 minutes. When the meat is white, chop it into bite-size pieces. Make sure there is no pink meat, if there is, heat it for another minute in the microwave.

Combine the butter, garlic, and vegetables, and microwave them for 3 to 4 minutes on high. Add the meat and cheese to the vegetables, spoon the mixture into each

tortilla. Sprinkle the quesadilla with shredded cheese, and microwave for 30 seconds. When the cheese is melted, it's ready to eat. Enjoy your snack!

Serves: 6   Prep: 7   Cook: 8   Total: 15

Tostadas Saborosas

This is one of the easiest recipes you are going to come across. If you can pile beans on a tortilla, you can handle this recipe. This is an especially good recipe for picky families, because everyone can make their own tostada, just the way they like it.

8 6-inch corn tortillas
2 tablespoons oil
1/2 cup refried beans
1 1/2 cups shredded cheddar cheese
2 cups shredded lettuce
1 cup chopped tomatoes
1/2 cup chopped onion
Black olives
Chilies
Sour cream
Taco sauce, or salsa

Dip a tortilla in oil and microwave it on high for 1 1/2 minutes. While microwaving, it should turn crisp. You can eliminate this first step by purchasing tostada shells instead of tortillas.

Spread the crisp tortilla with refried beans and microwave it for about 30 seconds. When the beans are hot, pile the tortilla with the toppings of your choice. Be creative, fix it however you want.

Repeat the process for each tortilla. Enjoy the tostadas.

Serve: 4 Prep: 2 Cook: 2 Total: 4

Peppy Pizza

Here's your chance to be really creative. Make your own pizza any way you like. This recipe is easy as pie; pizza pie that is. *(Photo on page 98.)*

1 6-inch Italian style pizza crust
1/4 cup pizza sauce or pesto
1/4 cup shredded mozzarella cheese
Toppings of your choice
1 tablespoon grated Parmesan cheese

Spread your pizza crust with either pizza sauce or pesto. Sprinkle on the shredded cheese. Top it with the toppings you like best. We'll even provide you with some suggestions: peppers, tomatoes, olives, onions, pepperoni, or sausage.

Sprinkle Parmesan cheese over the pizza and pop it in the microwave for 2 to 3 minutes. When the pizza is hot and the cheese is melted, your creation is ready to eat.

Serves: 1 Prep: 3 Cook: 3 Total: 6

Chicken and Pea Pods

Maybe you never make Chinese food because it just seems like too much work. Well, things are about to change. Here we have a recipe that can be nuked–no wok required.

1 tablespoon cornstarch
1/4 cup soy sauce
2 teaspoons fresh grated ginger root
2 1/2 pounds boneless, skinless chicken
   breasts cut into strips
2 6-ounce packages frozen pea pods
3/4 cup cashews

In a 2-quart casserole dish whisk the cornstarch into the soy sauce until it is dissolved and mixed thoroughly. Stir in the ginger root and microwave on high for 1 1/2 minutes. Add the chicken strips, cover, and microwave on high for 4 minutes.

Stir in the pea pods and microwave for 6 to 11 minutes. Stir the mixture every few minutes to break up the pea pods. When the meat is fully cooked and the pea pods are tender, stir in the cashews.

Now the dish is ready to serve. Dish the chicken over a bed of steamed white rice. Enjoy your meal. That was almost as easy as ordering out, right?

Serves: 6 Prep: 5 Cook: 15 Total: 20

Lemon Chicken

Chicken with a twist of citrus is very delicious, and worth trying. It takes a bit of time to make this dish, so start preparing about 45 minutes before you want to eat.

1 lemon
1/2 2-ounce jar thinly sliced pimentos
3 tablespoons olive oil
1 minced clove garlic
1 teaspoon basil
1/4 pepper
1 3-pound broiler-fryer skinned
   and cut into 8 pieces
1/2 cup chicken broth
1 tablespoon cornstarch dissolved
   in 2 tablespoons water
1/4 cup toasted bread crumbs
Lemon slices to garnish

Peel the lemon and chop the fruit. Squeeze 1/4 cup of juice from the lemon. Then combine the lemon juice, 2 tablespoons of oil, garlic, pimento, basil, and pepper. Arrange the chicken in a 2 1/2-quart casserole dish. Make sure the thickest part of each piece is toward the edge of the dish, then pour the lemon juice mixture over the chicken pieces. Slosh the chicken around so that the pieces are totally coated.

Add the broth to the chicken. Cover the dish, and microwave the chicken on high for 15 to 18 minutes. Microwave until the meat is white and the juices are clear. Rearrange the chicken pieces every few minutes, so they will cook evenly.

Stir in the dissolved cornstarch and microwave the dish of chicken on high for 3 minutes. The sauce should thicken slightly.

In a bowl combine the other tablespoon of oil, 1 teaspoon of shredded lemon peel, and the bread crumbs. Microwave on high for 2 minutes, and then sprinkle the mixture over the chicken. Microwave the dish for 2 more minutes. Let it stand for 5 minutes. Make a creative garnish with the lemon slices if you can think of something cool. Otherwise, just eat it and enjoy your meal.

Serves: 4 Prep: 17 Cook: 23 Stand: 5
Total: 45

BBQ Chicken

Perhaps the name is a little misleading. This barbecued chicken is cooked in the microwave of course, or it wouldn't be in this cookbook. It's so easy you may never go back to using the barbecue grill.

1 broiler-fryer
1/2 18-ounce bottle of your favorite barbeque sauce
Parsley for garnish

Wash and rinse the chicken thoroughly. Tuck the wings behind the bird, and place the chicken breast side up in a 12 x 8-inch casserole dish. Microwave on high for 10 minutes. Flip the chicken over and microwave it for 12 more minutes. The meat should be white and the juices should be clear. Let the bird stand for 5 minutes, and then drain off the juices.

Shake the bottle of barbecue sauce and pour it over the chicken. Use as much as you want, but 1/2 of the bottle is about what we recommend. Spread the sauce evenly over the surface of the chicken. Microwave on high for 5 or 6 minutes. The meat and the sauce should be hot.

Pull the chicken out of the microwave and garnish it with parsley. The parsley is just for looks, so if you don't have any, just skip it.

Serves: 4 Prep: 5 Cook: 18 Total: 23

Chicken Tenders

The good thing about this recipe is that the ingredients are easy to come by, in fact you may already have them in your kitchen.

2 tablespoons honey
1 1/2 teaspoons Dijon mustard
1 teaspoon orange marmalade
4 drops red pepper sauce
6 ounces breaded chicken chunks

Combine all of the ingredients, except the chicken. Mix them together very well, and microwave on high for 30 seconds, just until the sauce is hot.

Line a plate with paper towels and arrange the chicken pieces on it in a circle. Put another paper towel over the chicken pieces and microwave them for 3 to 5 minutes.

Turn the plate every minute. When the chicken tenders are hot, they are ready to be served with the sauce.

Arrange them on a plate and garnish with parsley if you have time. But if you're hungry, forgo the decorations and chow down.

Serves: 2 Prep: 2 Cook: 5 Total: 7

Chicken and Julienne Vegetables

In the summer, when zucchini and squash are plentiful, this recipe is an excellent dinner choice. Chicken and Julienne Vegetables is also a healthy choice because it's chocked full of healthy vegetables and chicken.

1/3 cup julienne carrots
1/3 cup julienne zucchini
1/3 cup yellow summer squash
1 boneless, skinless chicken breast, halved
Lemon pepper seasoning
Paprika
1/2 teaspoon dried parsley flakes
1/2 cup water

Butter Sauce:
1 tablespoon butter
1/4 teaspoon lemon juice
Dash lemon pepper seasoning

These directions aren't complicated, but they are a little different, so follow along carefully. Take 2 paper towels that are still connected. Lay it on a plate so that one square is centered on the plate, and the other side is off to the side. Combine the vegetables on the half of the paper towel that is sitting on the plate.

Top the vegetables with the chicken breast halves, and sprinkle them with lemon pepper, paprika, and parsley flakes. Fold the other half of the towel over so it's covering the vegetables and chicken. Pour the water over the towel to moisten. Fold the edges of the towel up around the vegetables and chicken, to form a little bundle. Microwave on high for 4 to 7 minutes, rotate the plate after a couple minutes. When the chicken feels firm, take it out of the microwave and let it stand for 3 minutes.

While the chicken and vegetables are standing, combine all the ingredients for the butter sauce in a glass cup. Microwave for about 1 minute, just until the butter is melted.

Unwrap the chicken and vegetable package and arrange everything on a plate. Spoon the butter sauce over the dish and serve.

Serves: 2 Prep: 8 Cook: 8 Stand: 3 Total: 19

Chicken Divan

Try our Chicken Divan when you want to make a balanced meal in minutes.

2 boneless, skinless chicken breasts
1 pound frozen broccoli florettes
1 10 1/2-ounce can cream of chicken soup
1/2 cup mayonnaise
1 cup shredded cheese
1/2 cup bread crumbs

Microwave the chicken breasts on a plate on high for 3 to 4 minutes. If the meat is finished it should be totally white. When the chicken is fully cooked, cut it into bite-sized pieces. Dump the frozen broccoli and the chicken pieces into a 9-inch pie plate.

Combine the soup, mayo, and cheese, and pour it over the chicken and broccoli. You don't need to stir it. Microwave on high for 9 minutes, rotating occasionally.

Take it out of the microwave and sprinkle it with bread crumbs. Let it sit 2 minutes, and then serve it. See—that was pretty easy, and just wait until you taste it, it's delicious.

Serves: 5 Prep: 5 Cook: 14 Stand: 2 Total: 21

Herbed Chicken

This chicken requires 6 hours to marinate. Other than that, it's a quick recipe. It takes less than 20 minutes to cook. So prepare it in the morning and enjoy a great chicken dinner that night.

3 pound broiler-fryer
1/3 cup white wine
3 tablespoons olive oil
3/4 teaspoon salt
1 minced garlic clove
1/4 teaspoon sugar
1/4 teaspoon dried tarragon
1/8 teaspoon dried mustard
1/8 teaspoon pepper

Place the chicken in a large nylon cooking bag, and put the bag in a dish. Set the chicken aside for a minute while you prepare the marinade.

Combine all the remaining ingredients in a bowl and mix thoroughly. Pour the marinade into the bag with the chicken, and tie the bag closed. Do one of those all-too-useful knots you learned in scouts and never got to use. Refrigerate for at least 6 hours. Leave it in overnight if it's easier.

After marinating the chicken, take it out of the bag, tuck the wings behind it's back, and place it on a roasting rack, breast side up. Microwave the bird on high for 10 minutes. Flip it over and microwave for 12 more minutes. The chicken is done when the meat nearest the bone is white, and if when you press it with a fork, the juices run clear. Let it stand for 5 minutes before serving.

The chicken is good served with rice or potatoes. And we know just where you can find some good potato or rice recipes. Just flip through this book.

Serves: 4 Prep: 3 Marinate: 6 hours
Cook: 19 Total: 6 1/2 hours

Chicken Cordon Bleu

Cordon Bleu takes a bit of preparation, but it's very good, and very elegant. So grab your meat pounder and get ready to have some fun. We know you'll love this delicious meal.

4 4-ounce boneless, skinless chicken breasts
4 thin slices ham
4 slices Swiss cheese
1/4 cup seasoned coating mix
1 teaspoon cornstarch
1/4 cup milk
2 tablespoons minced onions
6 sliced mushrooms
1/3 cup shredded Swiss cheese
Lemon peel garnish
Lemon pepper

Rinse the chicken breasts and pound each one until it is 1/4 inch thick. Place 1 slice of ham and 1 slice of cheese on each pounded chicken breast. Roll each chicken breast up like a sleeping bag, and secure with a wooden toothpick. Roll each chicken roll in the coating crumbs until completely covered.

Set each of the chicken breasts in a microwave-safe dish and microwave on high for 5 minutes. Turn the rolls over and microwave for 3 more minutes. When the chicken is cooked, pour the cooking juices into a cup, and set the rolls aside.

Dissolve the cornstarch into the milk, and stir it together until it forms a paste. Stir the paste mixture into the cooking juices. Then stir in the onions and mushrooms. Microwave the sauce on high for 2 to 3 minutes. Be sure to stir the sauce every minute. When it is thick and hot, stir in the cheese until it melts. Pour the sauce over each chicken cordon bleu. Microwave for 2 more minutes. Sprinkle with lemon pepper to taste. Garnish the meal, if you're striving to impress someone, and serve.

Serves: 4 Prep: 12 Cook 13 Total: 25

Honey Chicken and Rice

If you're looking for something healthy to make for dinner, stop here. Making this meal is a snap, so go ahead and try it.

1 teaspoon thyme
2 cloves finely minced garlic
2 teaspoons hot pepper sauce
1 teaspoon peanut oil
1/2 teaspoon red pepper flakes
1/2 teaspoon paprika
1 lime, juice and pulp
1 pound of chicken cut into
    bite-sized pieces
2 teaspoons honey
2 cups steamed rice
Parsley flakes

Dump the first 7 ingredients in a pie plate and mix them together. Toss the chicken in the spices and mix it around until all of the pieces are coated with the spice mixture. Arrange the chicken pieces in a ring in the pie plate so they will cook evenly. Microwave the chicken for 6 minutes. Be sure to turn the plate after 3 minutes. The chicken should be thoroughly cooked and white in the middle.

Immediately after cooking, dunk the chicken pieces in the honey. Let the honey chicken stand for 4 minutes before serving. That's about all it takes. Now you're ready to serve the dish with steamed white rice.

Serves: 4 Prep: 4 Cook: 6 Stand: 4 Total: 14

Parmesan Chicken

Try this family pleaser next time you need a quick meal. You can prepare it, cook it, and have it ready to serve in 20 minutes.

4 boneless skinless chicken breasts
1 egg
1 tablespoon olive oil
1/2 cup Italian-flavored bread crumbs
1/2 teaspoon crushed basil
1/2 teaspoon garlic powder
1/4 cup plus 2 tablespoons grated
    Parmesan cheese
4 slices mozzarella cheese
1 cup prepared marinara sauce

Wash the chicken breasts, pat them dry, and set them aside. In a pie plate whisk together the egg and oil. In another pie plate combine the crumbs, basil, and 1/4 cup Parmesan cheese. Take a chicken breast, dip it in the egg mixture, then roll it around in the crumb mixture until it is covered in crumbs. Do this with each chicken breast.

Arrange the chicken breasts in a baking dish and cover them with paper towels. Microwave the chicken on high for 7 to 9 minutes. Turn the dish around after 4 minutes. When the chicken is white all the way through it is done.

Place 1 slice of cheese on each piece of chicken, and then spoon 1/4 cup of marinara sauce over each piece. Do not cover the dish, and microwave it for 3 more minutes. When the cheese has melted and the sauce is hot, your quick meal is done cooking. Sprinkle each Parmesan chicken breast with Parmesan cheese, and your dinner is served.

Serves: 4 Prep: 8 Cook: 12 Total: 20

Cornish Game Hens with Rice

Really hungry? This is the meal for you. A cornish game hen, on a bed of hot brown rice will satisfy any appetite.

1 1/4 cups water
1 minced garlic clove
1 cup quick cooking brown rice
1/2 teaspoon dried leaf basil
2 22-ounce Cornish Game Hens

2 teaspoons margarine
1 1/2 tablespoons browning sauce

In a 2-quart microwave-safe casserole dish combine the water and the garlic. Microwave on high for about 5 minutes. When the water is boiling, stir in the rice and basil. Cover the dish tightly, punch the power down to 50%, and microwave for 10

minutes. After 10 minutes of cooking the liquid should be mostly absorbed.

Take the hens and wash them off. Pull out the guts and toss them in the trash. Arrange the hens over the rice with the meatiest part of each hen towards the edge of the dish. Set it aside for a minute while you make the browning sauce.

Chicken with Spinach Rice

Maybe spinach won't make you as strong as Popeye, but it's tasty stuff when prepared with chicken and rice. Try this recipe. It may become a favorite.

1 10-ounce package frozen
    chopped spinach
3 tablespoons butter
1 8-ounce package chicken-flavored rice
    and vermicelli mix
3 cups hot water
1/2 teaspoon poultry seasoning
1/4 teaspoon pepper
2 cups cut up chicken
1 8-ounce can sliced water chestnuts
1/3 cup almond slices

Unwrap the frozen spinach and place it on a plate. (Good luck getting it out of the box.) Once you have the frozen block of spinach on the plate microwave it on high for 5 to 6 minutes until it is defrosted. Drain the spinach and press on it to drain off as much water as possible.

Place 2 tablespoons of butter, rice, and vermicelli in a 2-quart casserole dish and microwave for 4 to 6 minutes. Stir every couple of minutes until the vermicelli is brown. Stir in the water, poultry seasoning, pepper, and the seasoning packet from the rice and vermicelli mix.

Microwave the rice on high for 5 to 10 minutes, stirring once. The mixture should thicken as it cooks, and the water should start to be absorbed.

Stir in the chicken, spinach, and water chestnuts. Mix everything well and microwave for 6 to 8 more minutes. The rice should be tender and all of the water should be absorbed. Set the casserole to the side for a few minutes while you prepare the nuts.

Place 1 tablespoon of butter and the almonds in a pie plate. Microwave them on high for 6 to 8 minutes, stirring them every couple minutes. They should be toasty golden brown when done. Sprinkle the nuts over the casserole, and it's ready to serve. Toss it on the table and dig in.

Serves: 6 Prep: 8 Cook: 32 Total: 40

(Cornish Game Hens continued.)
Melt the margarine in a little dish, by microwaving it for 30 seconds. Stir the browning sauce into the melted butter, and brush it over each hen. Cover the birds with wax paper and microwave them at 50% for 6 minutes. Then punch the power up to 70% and microwave for 6 more minutes. When the meat is white and the juices are clear, the birds are done cooking.

Let the dish stand for 5 minutes before serving. When it's ready, serve each hen over 1/2 of the brown rice, and see if that doesn't curb your appetite.

Serves: 4 Prep: 7 Cook: 18 Stand: 5 Total: 30

Hamburger Stroganoff

This stroganoff is the perfect dish for the picky family. There's nothing weird in it. Plus it's easy to make.

1 pound ground beef
1 tablespoon minced onion
1 10 3/4-ounce can condensed mushroom soup
3/4 cup milk
1 4-ounce can chopped mushrooms
1 tablespoon Worcestershire sauce
1/2 teaspoon garlic salt
1/4 teaspoon pepper
1 cup sour cream

Crumble the ground beef into a 2-quart casserole dish with the onion. Cover and microwave on high for 4 to 5 minutes. Stir the meat every couple of minutes, and break it into smaller pieces. Cook until the onion is tender, and the meat is no longer pink. Drain the grease off of the meat.

Stir in everything else, except the sour cream, and mix well. Cover the dish and microwave it for 5 to 6 more minutes. Stop and stir the mixture after about 3 minutes. The mixture should get hot and bubbly.

Stir in the sour cream until it is completely mixed in. Cover the stroganoff and microwave it for 1 more minute, just until it gets hot. Now your stroganoff is ready to be served over rice or noodles, you choose.

Serves: 5 Prep: 5 Cook: 12 Total: 17

Meat Loaf

Here we have one of the world's easiest dinners made fast. Making this Meat Loaf in the microwave tastes every bit as good as the traditional kind, in much less time. *(photo opposite page, bottom.)*

1 pound ground beef
1 egg
1/4 cup oats
1/4 cup onions
1 8-ounce can tomato sauce
1/4 teaspoon thyme
1/4 teaspoon marjoram
1 tablespoon brown sugar
1 teaspoon Worcestershire sauce
1 teaspoon prepared mustard

Mix together the ground beef, egg, oats, onion, 1/2 the tomato sauce, thyme, and marjoram. Using your hands is the most effective way, but if you really want to, you can use a spoon or something.

Get a 9-inch pie plate and set a custard dish or a cup upside-down in the middle of it. Mold the meat loaf into a ring shape around the cup. Form it so it doesn't touch the sides of the pie plate or the cup. Cover the dish with wax paper and microwave the meat loaf on high for 5 minutes. Pour the juices off of the meat loaf and set it to the side for a bit while you make the sauce.

Combine the rest of the tomato sauce, brown sugar, Worcestershire sauce, and prepared mustard. Pour the sauce over the meat loaf and cover it with wax paper again. Set the power at 50% and microwave it for 8 to 9 minutes. Turn the dish every few minutes so it will cook evenly.

Take the meat loaf out of the microwave, cover it with foil, and let it stand for 5 minutes. This is important because the meat continues to cook as it stands. When the meat loaf is ready to eat serve it with your favorite potatoes or rice. If you need a good recipe, there are some really tasty ones in this book.

Serves: 4 Prep: 6 Cook: 14 Stand: 5 Total: 25

Roasted Ribs

So you're craving ribs and you don't have a grill? No problem! You can nuke these savory roasted ribs. It's easy, just remember to rearrange them as they cook. You'll need about 1 pound of ribs per person. That might sound like a lot, but ribs are mostly bone you know.

3 pounds spare ribs cut into 3 rib pieces
1 thinly sliced onion
1/2 teaspoon basil
1 cup BBQ sauce
2 teaspoons lemon juice

Arrange the ribs in a 12 x 8-inch microwave-safe dish. Make sure the thickest parts are towards the outside of the dish. If you need to overlap any of the ribs, overlap the thinnest, least fleshy parts. Spread the onions over the ribs and sprinkle the basil on top.

Cover the ribs with wax paper to prevent grease from splattering all over the place and microwave on high for 5 minutes. Rearrange the ribs so they will cook evenly, and cover them with wax paper again. Punch the power down to 50% and microwave the ribs for 25 to 30 minutes. After 15 minutes, rearrange the ribs.

Drain the liquid from the dish and add the lemon juice and BBQ sauce. Microwave the meat uncovered for an additional 5 to 6 minutes.

Your ribs are now ready to eat. Watch out they are hot and gooey, enjoy, and don't forget to floss.

Serves: 3 Prep: 4 Cook: 40 Total: 44

Stuffed Pork Chops

Maybe you're wondering how you stuff a pork chop. It's not like there is really a place to put stuffing, right? Well, we'll tell you how to stuff a chop. It's a fun dish to serve, because it's not like you eat this sort of thing everyday.

4 pork chops
1/2 cup fine bread crumbs
1 cup sliced fresh mushrooms
1/2 cup chopped onion
2 tablespoons butter
1/4 teaspoon thyme
1 1/2 cups herbed-seasoned stuffing mix
1/2 cup hot water

Okay, pay attention because these instructions are pretty specific. First you need to slice the chops. Use a very sharp knife and slice the center of the pork chop to the bone, but leave a 1-inch border on the edges of each chop. Basically you're cutting a little cave area, or a pork chop pocket.

Now for the easy part. Combine the mushrooms, onions, and butter in a microwave-safe casserole dish, and microwave on high for 3 minutes, or until the onions are tender. Toss in the thyme and stuffing mix, and stir well. Microwave

the water on high for 2 minutes and add it to the stuffing mixture.

Poke about 1/4 of the stuffing into each pork chop pocket. Use a few wooden toothpicks to hold the opened end together. Dredge the stuffed chops through the bread crumbs. Dredging means to cover the chop with crumbs. The easiest way to do this is to dump the crumbs into a pie plate and roll the pork chops around until they are completely covered.

Arrange the chops in a microwave-safe baking dish with the bones towards the center. Cover the dish with wax paper and microwave at 50% for 15 minutes. Turn the pork chops over, re-cover with wax paper, and microwave them for 15 more minutes. Pork is done when it's white, so check the meat nearest the bone to see if it is fully cooked.

When the chops are done, serve them with your favorite side dish, and enjoy yourself. Remember to take the toothpicks out before eating.

Serves: 4 Prep: 8 Cook: 35 Total: 43

Sloppy Joes

This recipe is a kid pleaser. Parents will love it too, because it's fast and easy. When we say easy, we mean easy. It takes less than 15 minutes to make.

1 pound ground beef
3/4 cup diced onion
1 8-ounce can tomato sauce
1 tablespoon sweet pickle relish
1 teaspoon brown sugar
1 tablespoon cider vinegar
1 teaspoon Worcestershire sauce
1 teaspoon prepared mustard
4 hamburger buns
4 slices cheddar cheese

Combine the meat and the onions in a microwave-safe colander. Set the colander in a glass pie plate to catch the grease. Microwave on high for 4 to 5 minutes, or until the meat is no longer pink. Stir the meat mixture every 2 minutes so it will cook evenly.

In a 2-quart casserole dish combine the meat with all of the other ingredients, except the buns and cheese, of course. Stir everything together well, and microwave on high for 2 to 3 minutes. When the mixture is hot, it's ready to eat. Scoop 1/4 of the mixture on each bun, and top it with cheese. Serve these to your kids and see if they don't praise you.

Serves: 4 Prep: 5 Cook: 8 Total: 13

Glazed Ham

For parties or holidays, this glazed ham is just the thing to serve. The recipe feeds 10 people, but can easily be doubled for large groups or parties.

1/4 cup packed brown sugar
1 tablespoon prepared mustard
2 1/2 pounds fully cooked boneless ham

Put the ham in an 8 x 8-inch baking dish. Score the ham fat in diamonds. If you know what scoring is, skip to the next paragraph. If you don't know what scoring is, keep reading. Scoring is just cutting into the meat a little. To score the fat in

diamonds, just cut crisscrosses on the top of the ham.

Now stir the brown sugar and the mustard together thoroughly. Slap the glaze, which is the sugar-mustard mixture you just made, on the ham. Spread it evenly over the top of the ham.

Microwave the ham for 6 to 11 minutes, basting twice. Again, if you know what basting is, skip on. Basting is taking the juices from the bottom of the dish and drizzling them over the top of the ham. If you have a baster, you can use it to suck

the juices out of the bottom of the dish, and baste the ham.

When the glaze is set, it is finished. Cover the ham with foil and put it in the fridge. The ham is best when served cold, so make sure you prepare the ham enough in advance so you can cool it, usually the day before.

When it comes time to serve the ham, slice it and arrange it on a serving tray.

Serves: 10 Prep: 4 Cook: 11
Chill: 8 hours Total: 8 hours 15 minutes

Citrus Veal with Sage

This is basically a one-step meal. Even though it is not difficult, it is very elegant. This dish is a good choice for a quiet dinner.

1 pound veal scallopini sliced thinly
2 tablespoons lemon juice
2 tablespoons lime juice
1 teaspoon honey
1/2 teaspoon sage

1/2 thinly sliced lemon
1/2 thinly sliced lime

Combine the veal, juices, honey, and sage in a glass pie plate. Arrange the fruit slices over the meat. Cover the pie plate with plastic wrap and poke a couple holes in it with a fork. Microwave the meat on high for 4 to 5 minutes. When the meat is fully

cooked, take it out of the microwave and let it stand for 2 minutes. Remove the plastic wrap, chuck the fruit slices, and serve. See that was easy, yet elegant.

Serves: 4 Prep: 5 Cook: 5 Stand: 2 Total: 12

Beef and Vegetable Chow Mein

Don't let all these ingredients scare you off. This recipe has three basic steps and it's actually not that hard. Once you try it, this big oriental dinner will probably become one of your family favorites. Best of all this dish is very healthy.

1 pound ground beef
1 10 1/2-ounce can condensed beef consomme
2 tablespoons cornstarch
2 tablespoons soy sauce
1 teaspoon garlic powder
1/2 teaspoon ground ginger
1/4 teaspoon salt
1/8 teaspoon pepper
1 6-ounce package Chinese pea pods
1 thinly sliced onion
1/4 pound thinly sliced fresh mushrooms
1 thinly sliced celery stalk
1/2 pound fresh green beans
3 cups hot cooked rice

Crumble the ground beef into a microwave-safe casserole dish. Microwave on high for 5 to 6 minutes until the meat is no longer pink. Be sure to stir the meat after 3 minutes of cooking. Drain any grease off the meat, and set the beef aside for a bit.

In a glass bowl use a wire whisk to mix the corn starch and about 1/3 of the consomme. Stir vigorously until you have a paste-like mixture. Then add the soy sauce, garlic powder, ginger, salt and pepper and the rest of the consomme. Continue stirring it together until it is completely smooth and slightly thick.

Microwave on high for 6 to 7 minutes. Whisk the mixture every 2 minutes. The mixture should thicken as it cooks. It is finished cooking when it is thick and smooth. No lumps.

Pour the mixture over the cooked meat, add the pea pods, onion, mushrooms, celery, and green beans. Mix everything together.

Microwave for 5 to 7 minutes, stirring after 3 minutes. Toss in the sprouts, and microwave for 3 more minutes.

When the Chow Mein is heated all the way through, it's ready. Serve over a big pile of steamed white rice. If you're really hungry you might want to use a fork, but if you've mastered the art of eating with chop sticks— go ahead and enjoy.

Serves: 4 Prep: 6 Cook: 23 Total: 29

Tangy Round Steak

This is another one of those fun recipes that you cook in a bag. If you don't have a bag, you can still cook it in a dish. However you decide to cook it, make sure you try it. It's really good.

1 1/2 pounds boneless beef top round steak, cut 1 inch thick
1 tablespoon flour
1 thinly sliced onion
1 minced garlic clove
1/2 cup French dressing
1 tablespoon lemon juice
1 teaspoon Worcestershire sauce
1/4 teaspoon dried thyme leaves
1/8 teaspoon pepper

Put the flour in the bag and shake it around until the bag is coated with flour. Then stab the meat a few times with a fork until it is pierced thoroughly. Put the meat in the bag, and top it with the onion and garlic. Set the bag of meat aside for a minute.

In a bowl combine all the remaining ingredients. Pour the marinade over the steak and tie the bag closed. You don't have to tie a real fancy knot, just make sure the bag is tightly closed. Set the bag on a plate, and refrigerate for at least 8 hours. If you have the time, leave it in there overnight. Every few hours jostle the bag, and turn it over.

Later, after the meat has finished marinating, place the bag in a 9-inch baking dish. If you used a twisty to hold the bag closed, make sure there is no metal in it or you may see sparks.

Microwave on high for 5 minutes. Then punch the power level down to 50% and microwave for 30 to 40 minutes. After about 20 minutes turn the steak over. When the meat is tender it is finished cooking, but it's not ready to eat yet. Let it stand for 10 minutes.

Take the meat out of the bag, save the sauce. Place the steak on a serving plate, slice thinly, and serve it with the sauce.

Serves: 5 Prep: 15 Marinate: 8 hours
Cook: 45 Total: 9 hours

Cubed Steak with Fresh Vegetables

When you don't have forever to make dinner, but you want something filling and nutritious, this cubed steak and vegetables is the meal for you. In less than half an hour you'll be enjoying this delicious dinner.

4 cubed steaks
1 onion cut into 8 wedges
1 zucchini cut into 1/4-inch slices
1 tomato cut into wedges
2 tablespoons white wine
1/2 teaspoon dill

For anyone who doesn't deal with meat a lot, a cube steak is not just a square piece of meat, it's a certain cut. Look for meat that looks a bit like a hamburger patti. Place the cube steaks on a microwave roasting rack, and microwave on high for 6 to 8 minutes. Rearrange the steaks after 4 minutes. After the meat is fully cooked, drain off the grease.

In a microwave-safe bowl combine the onion, tomato, zucchini, wine, and dill. Cover the bowl and microwave it on high for 6 to 9 minutes. The onions and zucchini should be tender. Stir the vegetables every 2 or 3 minutes, so they cook evenly.

After the vegetables are tender, dump the mixture over the steaks. Spread it out evenly. Microwave the vegetable topped steaks for 2 to 3 more minutes. When the meat and tomatoes are hot, they are done. Arrange the vegetables and steaks on 4 dinner plates, and serve.

Serves: 4 Prep: 6 Cook: 21 Total: 27

Korean Sesame Beef

Hello, all you garlic lovers! You will love this dish. It's a no-oil-added version of Bul-kogee. It's easy to make, but allow some time for marinating.

1 tablespoon toasted sesame seeds
3 minced garlic cloves
1/2 teaspoon minced ginger
2 thinly sliced scallions
1 teaspoon soy sauce
1 teaspoon honey
1 teaspoon lemon juice
1 pound sirloin sliced thinly against the grain

In a 9-inch glass pie plate combine everything except the meat. Stir the mixture together well. Toss the beef in with the marinade. Make sure all of the meat is thoroughly covered with marinade. Cover the dish tightly with plastic wrap, and refrigerate for at least 1 hour. You can marinate it until you are almost ready to eat.

A couple of minutes before you are ready to eat, pull the meat out of the fridge. Make sure all of the meat is covered with marinade, poke a few holes in the plastic wrap with a fork and microwave on high for 5 to 6 minutes. Be sure to stir the meat every couple of minutes. When the meat is thoroughly cooked and hot, it is ready to eat. Serve with steamed white rice. Enjoy.

Serves: 4 Prep: 5 Marinate: 60 Cook: 6 Total: 71

Nice & Spicy Shrimp

Talk about easy. This recipe is as easy as they come. In just a few minutes you can whip up enough spiced shrimp to feed six hungry shrimp lovers.
(Photo opposite page, top.)

2 pounds raw, deveined, and peeled shrimp
1/4 cup butter
2 tablespoons flour
1 teaspoon parsley flakes
1/2 teaspoon coriander
1/2 teaspoon cumin
1/4 teaspoon salt
1/4 teaspoon pepper
1/4 teaspoon nutmeg
1/8 teaspoon cloves
1 1/4 cup milk

Spread the shrimp in a 2-quart casserole dish. Cover and microwave on high for 5 to 8 minutes, stirring the shrimp every 2 minutes. When the shrimp are pink and opaque (meaning not see through) they are done. So set them aside for a bit.

In a small dish, melt the butter by microwaving it on high for about 1 minute. Blend in the flour, parsley, coriander, cumin, salt, pepper, nutmeg, and cloves with a wire whisk. Stir until you have a smooth mixture. Then stir the milk in with the whisk. Microwave the sauce for 3 to 6 minutes. Stop the microwave and stir the mixture with a whisk every 2 minutes. When the sauce is thick, it is finished.

Drain the cooked shrimp and stir them into the spiced white sauce. Skewer the shrimp with cocktails picks, and enjoy!

Serves: 6 Prep: 2 Cook: 14 Total: 16

Shrimp and Pasta Toss

Linguine tossed with shrimp is the perfect meal for a summer evening. The key to making this dish is to use only the freshest of shrimp. *(Photo opposite page, top.)*

8 ounces uncooked linguine
1/4 cup olive oil
6 green onions chopped into 1/2-inch pieces
4 cloves minced garlic
2 pounds peeled and deveined shrimp
1/4 cup red wine vinegar
2 tablespoons lemon juice
1/4 cup chopped fresh parsley
1 1/2 teaspoons dried whole basil
1 teaspoon dried whole oregano
3/4 teaspoon salt
1/8 teaspoon pepper
1/2 pound fresh snow pea pods
4 peeled and chopped tomatoes
1/4 cup grated Parmesan cheese

Cook the linguine according to the package directions. While the noodles are cooking carry on with the rest of the recipe.

In a 2 quart casserole dish combine the oil, onions and garlic. Cover the dish with plastic wrap and microwave it for 3 minutes. When the onion is tender, stir in the shrimp. Mix until they are coated with the garlic mixture. Then arrange the shrimp around the edges of the dish and cover it with plastic wrap. Microwave on high for about 6 minutes. Stir every couple minutes. When the shrimp are pink they are done.

In a little bowl whisk together the vinegar, lemon juice, parsley, basil, oregano, salt, and pepper. After everything is mixed together well, stir the dressing into the cooked shrimp mixture. Toss the snow peas in and stir. Microwave for 1 minute, just until everything is hot. Stir in the tomatoes, and toss in the linguine.

After everything is mixed together, the shrimp pasta toss is ready to serve.

Serves: 6 Prep: 12 Cook: 10 Total: 22

Creamed Salmon

You can easily change this recipe into creamed tuna or chicken just by substituting tuna or chicken for the salmon. So choose your meat, and enjoy your dinner. *(Photo opposite page, bottom.)*

1 8-ounce package frozen peas in cream sauce
1 cup milk
1 tablespoon butter
1 7 3/4-ounce can salmon
1 4-ounce can chopped mushrooms

Empty the package of frozen peas in cream sauce into a 2-quart casserole dish. Add the butter and the milk. Microwave on high for 5 to 6 minutes. Stir every couple minutes. You should notice the sauce thickening. When the sauce is thick it is done.

Drain the mushrooms and the salmon, then dump the salmon and mushrooms in with the peas and sauce. Stir everything together and microwave for 2 to 3 minutes. After 1 minute, stir the mixture and scrape the sides of the dish. When the food is heated all the way through, take it out and serve over toast or pastry shells.

Serves: 4 Prep: 5 Cook: 8 Total: 13

Southern Style Catfish

If Huckleberry Finn had a microwave he probably would have fixed his catfish this way. It's a very fast and easy recipe for a tasty Southern favorite.
(Photo previous page, bottom.)

1/3 cup cornflake crumbs
1 tablespoon yellow cornmeal
1 teaspoon dried parsley flakes
1/2 teaspoon paprika
1/4 teaspoon salt
2 4-ounce catfish fillets
2 tablespoons milk

Combine the crumbs and spices in a pie plate, and pour the milk into a shallow saucer. Dip each fillet in the milk, and then roll it in the crumb mixture until the fillets are totally coated. Arrange them in a lightly greased baking dish. Make sure the thickest part of the fillet is towards the outside of the dish.

Microwave the fillets for 4 to 6 minutes. After 2 minutes flip them over and continue microwaving. The fish is done if it flakes when you cut into it with a fork. As soon as the fish is finished cooking, serve it with your favorite side dish.

Serves: 2 Prep: 3 Cook: 6 Total: 9

Scampi

You can make this scampi in a snap. If you buy shrimp that are deveined and shelled, it will only take about 5 minutes of preparation.

2 minced garlic cloves
2 tablespoons olive oil
3 tablespoons minced parsley
2 tablespoons dry white wine
1/8 teaspoon paprika
3/4 pound large shelled and deveined shrimp
1 1/2 tablespoons lemon juice
1/2 teaspoon salt
1/8 teaspoon pepper

Use an au gratin dish if you have one. It is a shallow oblong dish. If you don't have one, a casserole dish will work just as well. Combine the garlic and oil in whichever dish you end up using. Microwave it on high for 1 minute. Then stir in the parsley, wine, and paprika. Microwave on high for 2 minutes.

Dump the shrimp into the dish of spices and stir them until they are coated with the mixture. Sprinkle lemon juice, salt, and pepper over the shrimp mixture. Cover the shrimp and microwave on high for 2 to 3 minutes. Stir the scampi after one minute.

Toss the scampi onto your favorite pasta noodles, and dinner is served.

Serves: 2 Prep: 5 Cook: 6 Total: 11

Chick-n-Broc Quiche

This quiche is perfect for a brunch, or special breakfast. The chicken, broccoli, and eggs make it a fairly complete meal alone.

1 9-inch unbaked pie shell
1 whole chicken breast
4 slightly beaten eggs
1/4 teaspoon salt
1/8 teaspoon pepper
1 12-ounce package frozen chopped broccoli
1 cup grated Swiss Cheese
Slices of red bell pepper for garnishing

Put the pie crust into a microwave-safe pie plate. Poke holes in the bottom and sides of the crust with a fork. Microwave the crust on high for 3 to 4 minutes. When the pie starts to look dry, it is done cooking. Set the crust aside for a minute.

Defrost and cook the broccoli according to the package directions. Drain the broccoli and set it aside for a minute, too.

Rinse the chicken breast off and place it on a microwave-safe plate. Cover with wax paper and microwave it on high for 3 to 4 minutes. The chicken is done when it is no longer pink, and all the juices are clear. When the chicken is fully cooked, cut it into cubes and set it aside for a bit.

In a bowl, which doesn't need to be microwave-safe, combine all the ingredients except for the red pepper slices. Pour the mixture into the pie shell which should be slightly cooled by now. Punch the power level down to 50% and microwave the quiche for 9 to 11 minutes. When the quiche is set, it is finished cooking. Let it stand for about 10 minutes.

You can garnish the quiche with red peppers if you want. Then slice and serve it with juice, fruit, breakfast rolls, and all that good kind of stuff.

Serves: 6 Prep: 10 Cook: 20 Stand: 10
Total: 40

Denver Omelet

Apparently folks over in Colorado make omelets differently than everyone else. Maybe so. We decided to give you the recipe and you can decide if those people in Denver know the secret.

2 tablespoons butter
3 tablespoons diced ham
2 tablespoons diced green bell pepper
2 tablespoons minced onion
4 eggs
1/4 cup milk
1/4 cup shredded cheddar cheese

If you happen to have a microwave-safe omelet pan, use it. However, if you aren't a connoisseur of microwave-safe dishes, you can use a deep plate.

Measure the butter into the plate of your choosing, and microwave on high for 1 minute, or until it's melted. Stir in the ham, pepper, and onion. Microwave for 2 more minutes, making sure to stir after 1 minute. When the pepper and onion are slightly tender, pull the dish out of the microwave and set it aside for a minute.

In a bowl, whisk the eggs and milk together until blended. Pour this mixture over the ham mixture and microwave the whole dish on high for 3 to 5 minutes. Stir the omelet every minute until the eggs are slightly firm, but moist. Be really careful not to over cook the eggs. You don't want to make a rubber Denver Omelet.

Sprinkle the cheese over the omelet and microwave it on high for 1 minute, or however long it takes to melt the cheese. Now it's done, and you have made a Denver Omelet, right in your hometown.

Serves: 4 Prep: 7 Cook: 9 Total: 16

Scrambled Eggs

This is the way to make scrambled eggs. No frying pans or skillets necessary. All you need is a microwave and a little dish.

2 eggs
1/2 tablespoon butter
2 tablespoons milk

Melt the butter by microwaving it on high in a 2-cup casserole dish for 30 seconds. Crack the eggs into the melted butter, and add the milk. Beat the eggs with a fork until they are scrambled.

Microwave the eggs on high for 1 1/2 minutes. Stir them after 45 seconds. The eggs will still be a little wet, but don't microwave them any longer. Let the eggs set for 2 or 3 minutes, to finish cooking. When the eggs are firm, they are ready to eat.

Serves: 1 Prep: 1 Cook: 2 Stand: 3 Total: 6

Mexican Souffle

This Mexican Souffle makes a very delicious breakfast, but be sure to start the night before because it has to chill overnight. If you can crack an egg, you can fix this souffle.

6 slices white bread, cubed
6 eggs
1 teaspoon salt
Dash onion salt
1/2 cup melted butter
1 can green chili salsa
2 cups milk
1/2 cup shredded sharp cheddar cheese
Dash dry mustard
Dash cayenne pepper
1 can chopped green chilis

Crack the eggs in a large bowl and beat them with a wire whisk or egg beater. Set the eggs aside for a minute.

Pour the milk into a glass bowl and microwave it on high for about 2 minutes. Watch to make sure it doesn't boil over the top of the container. Add the heated milk, salt, and onion salt to the beaten eggs.

Rummage through your dish cupboard and find a 9 x 13-inch glass dish. Spread part of the bread on the bottom of the dish, sprinkle with cheese and chilis, pour on part of the egg mixture. Make another layer and pour the melted butter over the last layer of cheese. Cover the whole souffle with wax paper and refrigerate overnight, at least 8 hours.

Place the souffle in the microwave and cook on high for 10 to 12 minutes. Turn the dish every 3 minutes, but do not stir. Let the souffle sit for about 5 minutes before serving. If you're serving a nice brunch, try garnishing the souffle with peppers. Serve with green chili salsa on the side.

Serves: 4 Prep: 5 Chill: 8 hours Cook: 14
Stand: 5 Total: 8 1/2 hours

Desserts

Caramel Apples

What would Halloween be without Caramel Apples? This recipe is great for kids because it's super easy, and it's a lot of fun. So enjoy yourself, and be creative.

12 apples
12 wooden-popsicle sticks
2 14-ounce packages caramels
1/4 cup half and half
1/2 cup candy pieces or melted chocolate

Wash and dry the apples. Stab a wooden stick in the top end of each apple. Set the apples aside for a minute while you prepare the caramel.

Unwrap the caramels and place them in a 2-quart casserole dish with the half and half. Microwave on high for 5 to 7 minutes. Stir the candy every minute. When all of the caramels are melted, stir until they are smooth.

Place the candy pieces or the melted chocolate in another bowl. Dip each apple in the caramel sauce and set it on a piece of wax paper for a couple of minutes. Then dip each apple in the melted chocolate or roll it in the candy pieces. Be creative with the candy pieces, and have fun making these tasty caramel apples.

If the caramel begins to harden, reheat it in the microwave for a few more minutes. Let the apples cool until the candy is completely hardened. To speed up the process set them in the fridge or freezer. Store the apples in wax paper or cellophane.

Makes: 12 Prep: 10 Cook: 7 Cool: 30
Total: 47

Miss Jen's Cookies

Kids, this recipe is especially for you. These jumbo cookies are easy to make, and they are tons of fun to eat. But best of all they are huge.

3/4 cup shortening
1 cup packed brown sugar
1 egg
1/4 cup water
1 teaspoon vanilla
3 cups oats
1 2/3 cups flour
3/4 teaspoon salt
1/2 teaspoon baking soda
2 cups butterscotch chips, raisins,
    or candy pieces
1/2 cup chopped nuts
1/2 cup coconut

Put the shortening, brown sugar, egg, water, and vanilla in a bowl. Mix it with an electric mixer for about 1 minute. Everything should be a little fluffy.

Dump in the oats, flour, salt and baking soda. Stir it by hand a few times, and then beat it with a mixer until everything is well blended. Now you are ready to start cooking the cookies.

Cover a microwave-safe plate with wax paper. Take 1/2 cup of cookie dough and press it into a round cookie in the plate. The cookie should be about 4 inches across. Make sure the cookie is the same thickness everywhere.

Set the microwave at 50% and microwave 3 cookies for 2 minutes. When the cookies are done cooking sprinkle some candy or butterscotch chips on them. Wait a couple minutes for the cookies to cool, and then you can eat them with a big glass of milk.

For best results, only cook 3 cookies at a time.

Makes: 10 Prep: 10 Cook: 3 Total: 13

Pineapple Upside-Down Cake

This cake is actually rightside-up. If you have the pineapple on the bottom, then it's upside-down. Either way, it's easy. And whether you eat it rightside-up, or upside-down, it's very good.

1/4 cup butter
1/2 cup brown sugar
9 pineapple rings
9 drained and pitted maraschino cherries
1 box yellow cake mix

Mix half the cake mix according to the recipe on the box (enough for an 8 x 8-inch cake. Of course you can make the cake from scratch if you have all day. After you make the cake batter, set it aside for a minute.

Place the butter in an 8 x 8-inch microwave-safe dish. Melt it by microwaving it on high for about 1 minute. Sprinkle the brown sugar over the melted butter, and arrange the pineapple rings over that. Place one cherry in each pineapple ring.

Set a plate upside-down on the microwave floor and set the dish on it. This just helps the cake cook evenly. Microwave the pineapple on high for 1 minute. Spoon the cake batter evenly over the pineapple. Place the pan back on the upside-down plate, and microwave at 50% for 6 minutes. Rotate the pan every couple of minutes so the cake will cook evenly.

Set the microwave on high again, and microwave the cake for 6 more minutes. Sprinkle the cake with graham cracker crumbs, and let it stand for about 5 minutes. When you're ready to eat the cake, cut around the edges of it with a knife to loosen it. Then dump the upside-down cake upside-down on a rightside-up plate so that the cake is rightside-up. Enjoy your Upside-Down Cake.

Serve: 6 Prep: 10 Cook: 13 Stand: 5
Total: 28

Apple Crisp

This delicious baked apple dessert is topped with a crisp cinnamon and oat topping. That's why we call it Apple Crisp. Next time you have a few extra apples, try it, it's very good, and easy.

Topping:
1/2 cup sugar
1/2 cup brown sugar
1/2 cup flour
1/2 cup oats
1 teaspoon cinnamon
1/2 teaspoon nutmeg
1/4 cup butter

Apple Filling:
6 peeled and sliced apples
1 cup dried cranberries

Combine all of the dry ingredients in a bowl, and cut in the butter. This means stir the butter in with a fork or pastry cutter. Mix until the crumb mixture is pea sized. Set the topping aside for a minute while you prepare the apples.

Grease an 8-inch baking dish, and spread the apples and cranberries in the bottom of it. Sprinkle the topping over the apples.

Microwave the apple crisp on high for 14 to 16 minutes. Turn the dish after 7 minutes of microwaving. The apple crisp is ready to eat as soon as you pull it out of the microwave. It's especially good served with a big ol' scoop of vanilla ice cream.

Serves: 6 Prep: 10 Cook: 16 Total: 26

Granny's Gingerbread

This is a great recipe because all you do is dump everything in a bowl and stir. The bonus is that the molasses makes the bread dark, so no one will know that you cooked it in the microwave. *(Photo previous page, top.)*

1 1/4 cups flour
1/3 cup brown sugar
1/2 teaspoon soda
1/2 teaspoon salt
1/2 teaspoon cinnamon
1/2 teaspoon ginger
1/4 teaspoon cloves
1/3 cup shortening
2 eggs
1/3 cup molasses
1/4 cup hot water

Measure everything into a mixing bowl. Blend the ingredients on a low speed with an electric mixer. Then beat at medium for 2 minutes until thoroughly blended.

Pour the batter into a 8 x 8-inch microwave-safe dish. Microwave at 50% for 6 minutes, making sure to turn the dish every couple of minutes. Microwave the gingerbread on high for 3 more minutes.

Don't dig into the dessert for at least 5 minutes. Top it with whipped cream. We prefer it warm, but you can serve it any way you want.

Serves: 9 Prep: 6 Cook: 9 Stand: 5 Total: 20

Oh Fudge!

Christmas Candy making doesn't have to take forever. Since you're always rushed around the Holiday season, we are including this microwave fudge recipe just for you.

1 14-ounce can sweetened condensed milk
1 12-ounce package chocolate chips
1 teaspoon vanilla

Line an 8 x 8-inch pan with enough foil so it extends over the sides. Butter the foil thoroughly (don't freak out, this is fudge, it's not supposed to be healthy.) Set your dish aside for a minute.

Dump the can of milk and the chocolate chips into a microwave-safe container. Microwave these "extra healthy" ingredients on high for 1 to 2 minutes. Stir the concoction after 30 seconds. When the chocolate chips are melted, add the vanilla, and stir until completely smooth.

Pour the chocolate into the prepared pan, and chuck it in the fridge for a couple of hours, or until it hardens. Cut it into little squares and take it to all your friends at Christmas, or just eat it all by yourself; we don't mind.

Makes: 64 squares Prep: 6 Cook: 2 Cool: 120 Total: 128

Coconutty Bars

Are you looking for a treat that's sweeter than sweet? Try making these chocolatey, chewy, Coconutty Bars. They're very easy, and plenty sweet, so make sure you have at least one jug of milk on hand.

1/4 cup butter
3/4 cup graham cracker crumbs
1 14-ounce can sweetened condensed milk
1/2 cup semisweet chocolate chips
1/2 cup flaked coconut
1 cup chopped nuts

Place the butter in a 9-inch square baking dish and melt it by microwaving for 1 minute on high. Stir the graham crackers into the melted butter and press the crumbs to the bottom of the pan with your fingers or a cup, to form a crust.

Pour the sweetened condensed milk over the crust. Then sprinkle the chocolate chips and coconut over that. Cover the whole dish with half of the nuts. Press down slightly so the nuts sort of sink in a little.

Put a plate upside down in the microwave, and set the pan on the plate. Microwave at 70% for 8 or 9 minutes. Rotate the pan every 2 minutes. When the mixture is bubbly it is finished cooking. Sprinkle the rest of the nuts over the bubbly mixture and let it cool.

After about 30 minutes the bars should be cool enough. Cut the Coconutty Bars into squares, and serve them with lots of milk.

Makes: 24 Prep: 5 Cook: 9 Cool: 30 Total: 44

Peach Melba

This dish is easy and quick. It's fresh, tangy, and very delicious. Of course it's best when you use fresh peaches. Take a few minutes and try it.

4 halved fresh peaches
1 10-ounce package frozen raspberries
    or strawberries
1/2 cup fruit juice (apple, orange...)
1/2 cup raspberry jelly
1 tablespoon cornstarch
Vanilla ice cream

Thaw the frozen fruit (raspberries or strawberries) and save the juice. With a wire whisk stir the cornstarch into the juice you saved. When it's smooth stir in the other fruit juice (apple, orange...) and the raspberry jelly.

Microwave the mixture on high for 4 to 6 minutes, stirring the mixture every 2 minutes. It is done when it is slightly thick, about the consistency of gravy, but not lumpy gravy.

Toss the raspberries or strawberries into the microwaved sauce and serve over a big scoop of vanilla ice cream nestled in a peach half.

If peaches aren't in season, or if you prefer canned peaches they can be substituted. All you have to do differently is omit the cornstarch and use the peach juice in place of the 1/2 cup of fruit juice. Other than that the recipe is the same—easy.

Serves: 4 Prep: 3 Cook: 6 Total: 9

Ton-o-Chocolate Dip

If you're looking for something rich, creamy, and incredibly chocolatey you've found what you're looking for. Besides being irresistibly good, this Ton-o-Chocolate Dip is very easy to make.

2 tablespoons corn syrup
2 tablespoons butter
1 12-ounce package chocolate chips
1 cup half and half
1 teaspoon vanilla
Banana chunks
Pound cake squares
Pineapple chunks
Strawberries
Apple slices
Butter cookies

Put the chocolate chips and the half and half in a microwave-safe bowl. Microwave at 70% for 2 to 4 minutes. Stir the mixture every minute or so to avoid burning the chocolate. When the mixture is totally melted and hot, stir in the corn syrup and the butter until the mixture is smooth. Then stir in the vanilla, until it is totally smooth.

Transfer the dip to a serving dish, and arrange the banana chunks, cubes of pound cake, pineapple chunks, strawberries, apple slices, and butter cookies on a plate for dipping. Enjoy your rich, chocolatey treat. And no double dipping!

Serves: 8 Prep: 1 Cook: 4 Total: 5

Lemon-Chiffon Pie

This pie looks so lovely and tastes so great, that nobody will ever know how easy it is.

Crust:
1/4 cup butter
1 cup graham cracker crumbs

Pie Filling:
4 cups miniature marshmallows,
    or 40 large marshmallows
1/2 cup sugar
1/4 cup milk
1 tablespoon grated lemon peel
1/3 cup lemon juice
4 drops yellow food coloring (optional)
1 cup whipping cream

To prepare the crust, melt the butter in an 8-inch microwave-safe pie plate, by microwaving on high for 1 minute. Stir the crumbs into the melted butter. Use your hands or a cup to press the crumbs on the edges and bottom of the pie plate. Microwave the crust for 1 to 2 minutes, just until it becomes firm. Set the crust aside to cool while you continue with the recipe.

Combine the marshmallows, sugar, and milk in a microwave-safe bowl. Microwave on high for 2 to 3 minutes. Stir the melted marshmallows every minute. Stir the lemon peel, lemon juice, and food coloring into the mixture. The food coloring is just for looks, so you don't have to add it.

Let the mixture cool for about 30 minutes. When the mixture is stiff, stir the whipping cream into it. After stirring the cream in, the mixture should still be stiff. If it isn't let it stand in the fridge until it stiffens.

Scoop the filling into the pie crust you made earlier. Refrigerate the pie for an hour. Garnish the pie with lemon slices, and serve.

Serves: 8 Prep: 8 Cook: 3 Chill: 90 Total: 101

Southern Pecan Pie

Try making this quick pecan pie at Thanksgiving. We know you have enough to worry about with the turkey and all the fixin's, that's why we decided to include this easy microwave pecan pie.

1 premade uncooked pie crust
3 eggs
1/2 cup brown sugar
1 cup corn syrup
2 tablespoons melted butter
1 tablespoon flour
1 teaspoon vanilla
1/4 teaspoon salt
1 cup broken pecans

Separate 1 egg, and beat the egg yolk. Don't chuck the white, you'll need it later. Brush the pie crust with the beaten egg yolk. Microwave the crust for 1 minute. The egg should be set.

Mix the eggs and the previously separated egg white. Add the remaining ingredients, except for the pecans. Blend everything together well. Stir the pecans in and microwave on high for 3 to 4 minutes. Stir the mixture every 2 minutes.

Pour the hot mixture into the pie crust. Set the power level at 50% and nuke the pie for 9 to 13 minutes. Turn the pie half way around every 3 minutes. When the filling is completely heated and almost set, the pecan pie is finished cooking.

Serve the pie warm, or you can eat it cold if you can wait that long to start chowing down. Enjoy!

Serves: 8 Prep: 6 Cook: 18 Total: 24

Lime Pie

If you are convinced you can't cook, try making this dessert. You can prepare this chilled citrus pie in no time. It's easy and fast, not to mention very tasty.

1 9-inch chocolate cookie crust
1 1/2 cups water
1 3 1/2-ounce package lime gelatin
1/4 cup sugar
1/4 cup lime juice
2 teaspoons lemon juice
1 4 1/2-ounce carton frozen prepared
    whipped topping (thawed)
4 drops green food coloring (optional)

Bring the water to a boil by microwaving it on high. It will take 3 to 4 minutes. Stir the gelatin in until dissolved. Cover the dish and refrigerate the gelatin until it's partially set, about an hour.

Whip the gelatin until it's fluffy. As you whip add the sugar and the juices. Fold in the whipped topping. For everyone who doesn't know a lot about cooking, fold means to stir by hand until the topping is mixed in. If you want your pie to look really green, add about 5 drops of food coloring. This food coloring step is not a vital part of this recipe, so you can skip it if you want.

The pie needs to chill for about an hour before serving. If you're in a hurry you can put it in the freezer until it's cold, but don't forget about it. Garnish the pie with lime slices if you want, otherwise, just enjoy this great dessert.

Serves: 8 Prep: 5 Cook: 4 Chill: 120
Total: 129

Baked Apples

These cinnamony-sweet apples only take 10 minutes to cook. Try making these Baked Apples when you're looking for something new to make for dessert. People will think you worked all day to create such a tasty and appetizing treat.

4 apples (Granny Smith, Rome Beauty...)
Lemon juice
1/2 cup brown sugar
1/4 cup raisins
1/2 cup slivered almonds
1 teaspoon cinnamon
3 tablespoons butter
4 unwrapped caramels

Make sure you use baking apples in this recipe. Core and peel the top half of each apple. Arrange them in a baking dish, and splash each apple with lemon juice. Set it aside for a minute.

Combine the sugar, raisins, almonds, and cinnamon in a bowl. Stuff each apple with the mixture and one caramel. Dab 1/2 tablespoon butter on the top of each apple. Microwave the apples for 8 to 10 minutes. The apples are done when they are tender.

These apples are best when served with a massive scoop of vanilla ice cream.

Serves: 4 Prep: 8 Cook: 10 Total: 18

Crispy Marshmallow Treats

Everyone knows that making Crispy Marshmallow Treats is about the easiest thing to do. But we made it one step easier by using the microwave. This recipe is great for kids too.

4 cups miniature marshmallows
1/2 cup butter
5 cups crispy rice cereal
1 cup candy corn or gum drops

Grease a 9 x 12-inch baking dish with butter. Set it in a handy place, and continue with the recipe.

Dump the marshmallows and the butter into a big microwave-safe bowl. Microwave on high for about 2 minutes. Stir the marshmallows and butter every 30 seconds. Keep microwaving and stirring until everything is melted together and smooth.

Quickly dump in the cereal and the candy pieces. Stir until the marshmallows, cereal, and candy pieces are completely mixed. Try not to crush the cereal as you stir.

Lightly cover your fingertips with butter and press the mixture into the greased baking dish. About 15 minutes later when the Crispy Marshmallow Treats have cooled, cut them into squares and eat.

Makes: 24 Prep: 1 Cook: 2 Cool: 15 Total: 18

Scrumptious Cheese Cake

Simply delicious. That's about all there is to say about this rich creamy cake. Try any or all of the variations, you're sure to love them.

Crust:
1/4 cup butter
1 cup graham cracker crumbs

2 8-ounce packages cream cheese
2/3 cup sugar
1/4 teaspoon salt
1/3 cup milk
2 tablespoons lemon juice
4 eggs

Search through your collection of microwave-safe dishes and find a 9-inch round baking dish. If you don't have one, you can use a pie plate. Melt the butter in whichever dish you choose, by microwaving it on high for 1 minute.

Stir the crumbs into the melted butter, and press them evenly in the bottom of the pan. If you are using a pie plate, press the crumbs around the edges as well. Microwave on high for 1 1/2 minutes. Set the crust aside and continue.

Microwave the cream cheese on high for 30 seconds to soften. Beat the cream cheese, sugar, and salt together. Then blend in the eggs, milk, and lemon juice. Microwave the mixture in the bowl on high for about 4 to 7 minutes. Stir the mixture every couple minutes. When it's very hot, it's finished.

Pour the hot mixture over the crust and microwave at 50% for 7 to 15 minutes. Rotate the cake every 3 minutes. When the center of the cake is set, it's finished. Cool the cake, and then refrigerate it for 8 hours.

Garnish the cake or serve it with your favorite topping. Just make sure you enjoy it.

Now for the variations.

To make a Toffee Crunch Cake, crush 4 chocolate covered toffee bars and sprinkle them over the cake 3 minutes before it's finished cooking.

Make a Christmas Cheese Cake by sprinkling a cup of crushed peppermint candy over the cake 3 minutes before it's finished cooking.

To make a Chocolate Cheese Cake, sprinkle the cheese cake with 2 cups of chocolate chips immediately after it finishes cooking.

For fruit cheese cakes, spoon thawed frozen fruit, canned pie filling, or fresh berries over the cooled cheese cake.

Serves: 8 Prep: 7 Cook: 25 Chill: 8 hours
Total: 8 1/2 hours

Carrot Cake & Cream Cheese Frosting

The best thing about making this cake is that it only takes 15 minutes to cook. Nobody wants to wait forever while the cake cooks. That's why we included this speedy carrot cake recipe.

1 1/2 cups flour
1 1/2 teaspoons baking powder
1 1/4 teaspoons baking soda
3/4 teaspoon salt
3 teaspoons cinnamon
1/2 teaspoon cloves
1 1/2 cups sugar
1 cup oil
3 eggs
2 cups grated carrots
1 8 1/2-ounce can crushed pineapple
1/2 cup chopped walnuts

Combine all the dry ingredients. Add in the sugar, oil, and eggs. Mix until the ingredients are thoroughly blended. Stir in the carrots, pineapple, and nuts. Stir until everything is mixed together.

Find your microwave-safe bundt pan or tube-cake pan. Read the manufacturer's instructions on greasing. If you can't locate the instructions, grease and flour the pan just to be safe.

Pour the batter into the prepared cake pan. Microwave the cake on high for 10 to 12 minutes. After cooking, let the cake cool for 5 minutes before placing it on a wire rack to cool completely. This cake is best frosted with our Cream Cheese Frosting on the next column.

Serves: 8 Prep: 8 Cook: 12 Total: 20

People have been known to eat carrot cake just for the rich cream cheese frosting. This frosting is that good. If you eat the cake just for the frosting, we understand completely.

1/4 cup butter
1 3-ounce package cream cheese
2 cups powdered sugar
1 teaspoon vanilla
1/3 cup milk

Are you ready? This is really easy. Put everything in a bowl. Microwave it on high for 30 seconds to 1 minute. Beat the frosting until fluffy. You probably ought to taste it a couple times just to make sure it's good enough to serve.

If it passes the test, frost your favorite cake with it, and enjoy.

Frosts: 1 cake Prep: 4 Cook: 1 Total: 5

Index

Dear Cardholder,

Happy Anniversary! This gift is our way of thanking you for being part of Prime Option MasterCard this past year. It truly is a gift, a present, that we want you to enjoy. We hope, however; that each time you use it, you will think of Prime Option and all of the wonderful features we offer to you our Cardholder.

Here's why we selected a cookbook as our anniversary gift. We wanted a gift that would represent our credit card. We feel, and we hope you agree, that the Prime Option MasterCard card is a well-used and convenient tool, much like a microwave cookbook. Secondly, we know that everyone needs to eat, but not everyone can spend much time making food. And finally, we know most people have microwaves, but most of them only use them to heat leftovers or pop popcorn.

With this information we decided it would be a great idea to make a microwave cookbook filled with plenty of options for making speedy meals. We hope the cookbook proves to be as useful as your Prime Option MasterCard.

Making this cookbook was quite a process. We started by hiring some cooks and artists to help make this a beautiful book. We then volunteered ourselves to do the taste testing. Well, someone had to do it! We found the recipes so tasty that we celebrated the completion with an office cookbook party. Everyone cooked one recipe from the Prime Option Cookbook, and brought it to our big pot luck feast.

Our objective was to include tasty, yet easy-to-follow recipes. Anyone from college students to experienced cooks will have fun with the many options in this cookbook. And while you may not garnish your meals with flowers and creatively-cut vegetables, we think you'll be pleased as you discover the potential of your microwave.

For all you microwave antagonists out there, be assured that almost any of these recipes can be adapted to your stove top or conventional oven.

Much like our goal with the Prime Option MasterCard, our aim is to provide you with a useful, innovative, and enjoyable tool. So feel free to use the recipes in whatever way suits you best. Also for your convenience, remember that many grocery stores now accept your Prime Option MasterCard, so you can easily use your card to purchase the foods you'll need to try all these tasty cookbook options in your microwave.

We look forward to a long relationship with you as a Prime Option MasterCard Cardholder. Happy Anniversary!

Best Wishes

J. M. Childers
Senior Vice-President, Marketing

THE
SIMPLY DELICIOUS OPTIONS
MICROWAVE COOKBOOK

Your Gift From | Prime Option℠ MasterCard®

D1711853